A Requiem

to the

Vitality

of

Life

Echo Klaproth

ISBN 978-1-0980-3069-8 (paperback)
ISBN 978-1-0980-3070-4 (digital)

Christian Faith Publishing, Inc.
832 Park Avenue
Meadville, PA 16335
www.christianfaithpublishing.com

Cover Photo © 2019 Don Anderson, Riverton, WY

Printed in the United States of America

During two of the most difficult seasons of our lives,
my family was blessed by the care provided from hospice teams.
As a result of those seasons, that care, hospice became my calling
and I joined a nonprofit organization, first as a volunteer
and then later as their chaplain.
It is through the observations over several years
and the collective presence and ways so many chose
to live out their life or to care, give, and support another
human being as he or she finished their time here on earth
that I've come to a better understanding of the vitality of life.

It's them and their stories that I shall always be grateful for
and remember. This then is a collection of reminiscences
about the process of not only living out but finishing life
that's been humbly recorded in prose and poetry in their honor.

Heaven awaits after
the winding and dangerous road
of untold suffering,
unanswered questions,
unmet dreams,
and unfulfilled hopes.

"Requiem aeternam dona eis, Domine.

Grant them eternal rest, O Lord."

On a Personal Note

"Truly, truly, I say to he who hears My word
and believes Him who sent Me,
has eternal life and does not come into judgment
but has passed out of death into life."

—John 5:24

An Introduction: Learning to Die

I don't know how you do it. I know I couldn't do what you do!

It's an observation often spoken. And while I don't have a pat answer, it's my hope that the stories contained in these pages will help others of you understand. I didn't choose to be a minister for the dying; it was a calling from God. And because of where I am physically, emotionally, and spiritually—older and a wee bit wiser after having surrendered my life to Jesus—the calling on my heart and the ministry that has come with that call is what led me to the subsequent writing about experiences with those in the throes of living and dying that has forever and dramatically changed my thinking about the vitality of life. To quote an unknown author, *"All my life I thought I was learning to live; but now I realize I was learning to die."*

I grew up a rancher's daughter. We experienced life and death daily through our humanness but especially through all of nature. What I learned through the growing up process is, we humans tend to take life for granted and consider it commonplace; that is if we give it any consideration at all. In agriculture, we experienced death daily through nature and the seasons; however, it was only commonplace because we came to experience it as a natural part of the cycle of life. Unfortunately, it takes some living to understand that while death might seem ordinary on one level, it uniquely hits home and becomes personal when it involves someone we love, or becomes our reality through a diagnosis. Despite whether we know and admit death is inevitable at some level or not, most of us are never ready. Scripture tries to prepare us by saying it in this way, *"For you yourselves know full well that the day of the Lord will come just like a thief in the night"* (1 Thessalonians 5:2).

As a hospice agent, I am reminded of this truth repeatedly, but at one particular funeral, the thought came, *"No truer statement has ever been spoken about life."* The minister asked that no credit be given to him, so I simply begin this collection of writings with his thoughts: *"Death teaches us so much more than life. Death is commonplace until it hits home or takes someone we love. Then it becomes painfully original, new, and unusual. We're never ready."*

As a Christian, I believe that the times of our lives are in God's hands, *"My times are in Your hand…make Your face shine upon Your servant; save me in Your lovingkindness"* (Psalm 31:13–16). It's been my personal experience that He comes alongside and walks us through the occasions of living and dying while on earth because it's the significance of being mortal. *"Even though I walk through the valley of the shadow of death, I fear no evil, for You are with me"* (Psalm 23:4). There is hope, however, and it's through the name of Jesus who promises, *"Truly, truly, I say to you, he who hears My word, and believes Him who sent Me, has eternal life, and does not come into judgment, but has passed out of death into life"* (John 5:24).

As a writer, I have found I can't not write; words come tumbling out at random times, in random order, for random reasons. It was after becoming a hospice chaplain that the focus of my writing transformed and became more frequently and in particular about people in the process of living out their time on earth. Being with and observing people as they face the end of and finish their life can have a variety of effects on the human psyche. What I have found is, it is about living, about love, about patience and endurance, and about faith in God. And so this collection will be about learning to and living with the truth that we are all going to die. For some, it's simple—you live your life and then you die—end of the story. For others, death is a painful and abhorrent concept and the suffering is heart-wrenching. Yet others have shown that with patience, endurance, and faith in a loving Savior, it can be a tender and beautiful experience.

Love is core to this book, is core to the stories. The concept of "love" and all the word entails is brought to light through relationship. Dr. Karen M. Wyatt, author of *What Really Matters*[1] wrote, "Relationships create a situation in which we must balance our own hopes and desires with those of another person and are therefore full of ups and downs, conflicts, and challenges (pg. 52). "Because our minds have been trained to focus on either our memories of the past or our dreams of the future…the mind excels at rewriting the past and inventing the future…we are suspended between them on a slender thread upon which we must balance" (pg. 75).

I've remained suspended on a slender thread, balancing between do I tell the stories/do I not tell the stories? It remains a valid question in my heart. However, throughout the process of saving the stories and then putting this collection together, there were several friends, co-workers, writers, and family members who encouraged the proposal and even contributed to individual stories. Thank you to Imy Eager and her family who not only supported the idea, but gave me permission to use Jim's eulogy and poem; Julie Smith, Sue Franks, DeeDee Nida, and members of Westword Writers listened, edited, and offered constructive criticism. Thank you all for the shows of support and encouragement. And I offer a special thank you to Rick, the one who listens to all the stories and helps me keep my intentions centered around love.

This collection reflects the stories of real people: those balancing between "the bonding with the innocent and vulnerable child that still exists within each of us that leads people to die the way they've lived" (Wyatt, pg. 145); those who fought a hard battle but found they weren't in control all along; those who grieved the fact that they were born in the first place—those living life to the fullest, those who chose to go out kicking and cussing their fate, those who touched our lives and left such an impact that we remember them above all others. Names will not be used; it's the stories that are key and all the nuances that the effort of living and dying entail because it's been my experience that it's the same for all of us, whether we recognize or acknowledge it or not:

> *"All my life I thought I was learning to live; but now*
> *I realize I was learning to die."*

[1.] What Really Matters, by Karen M. Wyatt, MD.

Doing Unto Others

James 1:22

You can begin by listening
to the stirrings in your heart,
those that speak, "Reach out."
Become a doer of the Word,
not merely a hearer and touch
first with a word of compassion
that reflects "love one another."
Next move your feet forward
and step into and taste the fear:
"I don't know what to say to them."
As you swallow that bitter pill,
be reminded how you might like
to be treated if it was you
trying to digest a terminal diagnosis.

Faith in Action

"For I know the plans that I have for you," declares the LORD,
"plans for welfare and not for calamity to give you a future
and a hope. Then you will call upon Me and come and
pray to Me, and I will listen to you. You will seek Me and
find Me when you search for Me with all your heart."

—Jeremiah 29:11–13

My first and perhaps hardest lesson with regard to the vitality of living and finishing life and hospice care came from a thirty-six-year-old. Because of his age, back story, and our relationship, his was especially hard. He wrestled with alcoholism and drug addiction much of his young life and had been granted more than one second chance at life after a couple car wrecks and an accidental drug overdose. Then along came love and he was finally able to quit it all, "cold turkey." The right and perfect woman loved and encouraged him in his sobriety and faith. He adopted her daughter and was button-popping proud with the births of his son and daughter. It seemed he finally had a purpose, something to live for. Life was looking promising.

He woke up one morning with a lump the size of a nerf football on his neck. Initially thought to be lymphoma, tests proved it to be melanoma. Time proved it to be relentless. He was stunned. He was sad. He kept working as best he could, continued to take in the days as best he could, turned to his faith and clung to his wife and his hope.

12

As his oldest sibling and the only girl, my earliest recall is age five and the day they brought him home. I thought he was my very own baby doll. Characteristically from then on, I was the one who came alongside my youngest brother's side. After his diagnosis, I drew up alongside my sister-in-law, attempted to become her buffer: was the one who relayed news to other family members; was the one praying and trying to console our mother and other brothers; was the one helping with his precious children, trying to be present for it all while he was busy fighting for dear life. He was determined to live.

He volunteered to try a new drug being tested, but when the team at University Hospital told him there was no more they could do for him, he said, "I want to go home to die." I drove home to see what options were available. His wife didn't want the children's last memories of their father to be dying in a hospital bed in their living room, so I went to the local hospital. The administrator told about a hospice room on the second floor: a room down a quiet hallway that looked less like a hospital room and more like a family's sitting room: there were recliners and none of the hospital smells or buttons and buzzers were present; it was a place where family and friends could gather and stay, where coffee and cookies magically appeared at all hours; and most importantly, nursing care was available 24-7. It was a place where my brother would be kept safe, comfortable, and reasonably pain free. It was an answer to prayer.

By this time, he had wrestled with the demons of: questions without answers, doubt, anger, fear, frustration, the reality that he was dying and there wasn't a thing he could do to control or stop it. The rest of us mostly functioned in disbelief and non-reality, but he rose to the occasion with a strength and calm courage that we'd not ever observed in him before. As a rancher and farmer, he was well aware of the cycles of birth and death in all of nature. But to date, we had only lost grandparents and a father, all older and as expected in the natural cycle of things. His situation was an enigma—why now, why so young, why this way, why after he had finally figured out what was important in life?

It seemed that while life was being sucked out of him, painfully slowly but surely, in actuality, life was being satisfied through and in him. He had turned his life over to Jesus some time before the cancer, but it was the cancer that drew him closer than ever to Him who *"knows the plans that I have for you…"* (Jeremiah 29:11). It was the cancer who helped my brother recognize and acknowledge once and for always, *"You are my hope; O Lord God, You are my confidence"* (Psalm 71:5). In the end days, it was to Jesus that he cried out. Our last good conversation the day before he died was a telling one. In a moment of clarity he looked right at me and when I asked what he needed, he spoke clearly, "I need you to quit smoking, you have too much to live for."

It was the cancer that had rendered his body helpless, but it was God and my brother's faith in Him that rendered the cancer powerless. Faith gave my brother the strength to endure five surgeries, a multitude of different treatments, and in the end gave him the strength to die, knowing that heaven was before him. Faith saved his life, and mine, and perhaps others around us during that time and trial: *"and though you have not seen Him, you love Him, and though you do not see Him now, but believe in Him, you greatly rejoice with joy inexpressible and full of glory, obtaining as the outcome of your faith the salvation of your souls"* (1 Peter 1:8–9).

A community drew together in support of our extended families and the blessings abounded around us and embraced the pain and grief. My little brother's faith, that from Hebrews 11:1, "Now faith is the assurance of things hoped for, the conviction of things not seen" is his legacy and what most especially defined what living and finishing life is all about for me and others who loved him. His was a most precious gift of life to those of us who observed faith in action.

The Story of a Son with a Purpose

"And we know that God causes all things to work
together for good to those who love God,
to those who are called according to His purpose."

—Romans 8:28

As I searched for words for that day, I looked for those that would best honor my firstborn son and the man he had become. Plus, I wanted to find words that might help provide peace and understanding for his siblings, his wife and two young sons, other members of our family, and indeed all who were grieving his death. I suppose it was a natural that I was lead to the Book of John—the story of a humble but dedicated, sincere, and hardworking man.

John the Baptist was a man who believed his purpose in life was to witness and teach mankind about Jesus, about faith, about miracles, about the Resurrection, and about eternal life. John never laid claim to anything else. Many thought he was the Messiah. However, when asked, *"Who are you?"* John simply replied, *"I am the voice of the one calling from the desert—make straight the way to the Lord"* (John 1:23). He was an unpretentious man who carried out his purpose in life with grace and truth.

Just as John the Baptist, our son never claimed to be more than who he was: son, brother, nephew, cousin, husband, father, co-worker, team member, friend, and a child of God. And while in a much less notable way, he too felt he had a purpose in life. One night not long before he died, he shared with me that he'd known for a long time—even since childhood he said—that he'd been called to do work for God. And so when he learned he had cancer, he determined, "This [the cancer] is my purpose." He believed it so fervently that he said it is what gave him strength over four tumultuous years.

Now, that didn't mean that he didn't question, or that he always handled his illness with goodwill. No, he was human. It was important that we remember that he did question, sometimes did curse this "lot in life," was sometimes angry. He had reason, he was only thirty-three years old; he was happily married to the love of his life, had two small sons he adored, and his life's dreams and plans had been suddenly and inexplicably altered. Yet he never quit believing in the possibility of recovery, and he was never once heard to ask, "Why me?" In fact, a devout Catholic, he experienced being born again through Christ weeks before his passing. To him that meant he was forgiven of his sins and was granted an even more intimate relationship with God.

Through it all, he remained aware of God's spirit working through him: he witnessed, struggled, and taught lessons about tolerance, loyalty, mental, physical, and spiritual strength, and perseverance through his biggest challenge in life. As a competitive person, he had always expected the best out of himself. The rest of us, family and friends, ran frantic, spent hours grieving and speculating. We let precious moments go unnoticed, left unsavored. That is until we heard, "The tumor has grown."

Suddenly we faced the reality of cancer and life. We watched him square his shoulders. Each moment became a precious entity because we were no longer sure how to measure time. Each day was a gift, and we began to open the quiet moments of everyday life. We unwrapped and celebrated small graces at any opportunity. We rejoiced in every hug, every smile, and each day spent together snuggled in the warmth and love of family and friends. We sang new songs, and we danced in the kitchen.

Meanwhile, he kept teaching lessons about forgiveness, resolve, bravery, and he witnessed how to hold one's head high when facing adversity. At his funeral, I shared a quote from a book called *Small*

Graces by Kent Nerburn who wrote, "We dream our lives in grand gestures, but we live our lives in small moments." My son helped us learn that we tend to worry about temporary things when all we truly need do is believe in God for who He is and what He promises and then believe in ourselves through His promises. He showed us how to do the best we can where we're placed, with the burdens we're handed. In no uncertain terms, he taught us to sanctify the ordinary and do it with purpose! We believe he asked for and received eternal life through his deep, abiding faith in Jesus Christ.

"But even if you should suffer for the sake of righteousness, you are blessed. And do not fear intimidation, and do not be troubled, but sanctify Christ as Lord in your hearts, always being ready to make a defense to everyone who asks you to give an account for the hope that is in you, yet with gentleness and reverence..." (1 Peter 3:14–15).

From Another Angle

"The concept of 'love' and all it entails is brought to light
When working with those who are at the end of life."

—Author Unknown

A Parable about Death

There was this man who was sitting at home, minding his own business, when he heard a knock at the door. He opened the door and found a man standing there who introduced himself as Death. After he told the man why he had come, the man said, "No, this has got to be some kind of a mistake; it's not my time yet. This can't be right." Death double-checked the address, asked the man his name, and replied, "No, I'm at the right place."

It shook the man in a mighty way and he simply couldn't wrap his head around this strange turn of events. Only moments ago he'd been sitting in his living room with his family, minding his own business. To stall things a bit, he invited Death in for a cup of coffee, and Death agreed and followed him into the kitchen. As the coffee perked, the two quietly studied one another. When it was ready, the man decided to try to buy some time and sprinkled a little sleeping powder in Death's cup of coffee. It worked. Before very long, Death laid his head over on the table, fast asleep.

It was then the man noticed a piece of paper sticking out of Death's pocket, so he took it and saw that it was a list of names, with his being the first. He quickly erased his name and rewrote it at the bottom of the page before returning the paper to Death's pocket.

Thinking himself very clever, he smugly sat waiting for Death to awaken. When Death did come to, he said, "You know, you have been so gracious to me this afternoon, I've decided I'll leave you alone and go visit the name on the bottom of the list."

Dignity Defined

Dignity defined stands alone as: integrity, respect, and compassion. It's a primal social covenant, *"so that we may lead a tranquil and quiet life in all godliness and dignity."*

—1 Timothy 2:2

From his book, *The Best Care Possible*, Ira Byock, MD, says, "Human beings belong to one another before we are born and long after we die. In a morally healthy society, people are born into the welcoming arms of the human community and die from the reluctant arms of community. Within this covenantal experience, the well-being of others affects my own quality of life." He adds further that it's an "ethical framework which encompasses whether and to what extent society first must meet the basic human needs that people have as they approach life's end. Basic elements of human care underpin how we regard and respond to others as people become sicker and more physically dependent" (pg. 283).

As a contributor to and a participant in hospice and home care, the goal of our team is to provide a supportive environment where a person's dignity can be maintained as best as is humanly possible. Considered to be the model for quality, compassionate care for people facing a life-limiting illness or injury, hospice care involves a team-oriented approach to expert medical care, pain management, and emotional and spiritual support expressly tailored to the patient's needs and wishes. That same support is provided to the patient's loved ones as well.

The decision to seek hospice care ultimately rests with the patient, and his or her family members are encouraged to discuss the need for hospice care with their physician, health care team, clergy, and friends. Comfort care and dignity are the center of hospice and palliative care. Hospice teams include professionals specializing in end-of-life maintenance: doctors, nurses, CNAs, care coordinators, social workers and bereavement counselors, spiritual counselors, administrators and office staff. With dignity as the standard, staff members attempt in every way to make and keep the patient's care safe, clean, comfortable, and convenient as possible, with respect and compassion as the leading guideline.

A Song That Never Ends

"But the one who endures to the end, he will be saved."

—Matthew 24:13

Sometimes the "songs" that our clients and their families sing comes from an overflow of joy and gladness. It seems that God had opened up heaven and overflowed their hearts with His blessings. The result is a peaceful refrain of contentment that spills out of them as an effortless melody, heaven's embrace flowing from within: *"Having loved His own who were in the world, He loved them to the end"* (John 13:1).

At other times, we find ourselves in the midst of a dark night narrative, listening to the blues sung stinging and abrasive by someone who is afraid and lacking hope—suffering's song. It is at those times that we cling to Exodus 15:2, *"The LORD is my strength and song, and He has become my salvation..."*

I am unified with a team of people who are equally dedicated to caring for others with a chorus of comfort and love; we serve those as servants of the Most High who calls us to the work of caregiving. And when another human cries out in pain of any kind, we attempt to become a sheltering place, a sanctuary from the troubles that weigh them down. We offer melodies from our hearts, surrounding them with love articulated through the lyrics of a well-known song:

> *Love is a song that never ends*
> *Life may be swift and fleeting*

Hope may die yet love's beautiful music
Comes each day like the dawn
Love is a song that never ends.[2]

Scripture, Ephesians 2:10 in particular conveys that we are God's **workmanship**—translated from the Greek **"poiema."** We are God's poem and there's a song that He wants to sing through each of us. First John 4:7 reminds us: "Beloved, let us love one another, for love is from God; and everyone who loves is born of God and knows God." That's what we have come to hope, trust, walk in, and sing, despite from where or how our clients come to us. And it's my prayer that we always sing the song of love that is never ending.

[2.] "Love Never Ends" by Crystal Bernard.

We Are His Poem

Ephesians 2:1–10

I'm just a pen that was designed
to write the words to serve mankind,
but you're the lyrics laced throughout,
completing the song as Christ's devout.
And it's by grace that we've been saved—
not by our works but what He forgave.
Prepared in advance for His home,
a gift from God, we are His poem.

Not from ourselves but through our faith
in Christ Jesus He did create
a merciful song, chords divine—
sung from above, His will be thine.
And it's by grace that we've been saved—
not by our works but what He forgave.
Prepared in advance for His home,
a gift from God, we are His poem.

God wrote us to sing, to impart
rhymes and rhythms that mirror His heart.
It's through Jesus that we're alive
and it's through Him that we'll survive.
And it's by grace that we've been saved—
not by our works but what He forgave.
Prepared in advance for His home,
a gift from God, we are His poem.

Laying Down One's Life

"Greater love has no one than this:
to lay down one's life for a friend."

—John 15:13

I don't know how many times I had either read or heard Jesus's words referenced through a teaching about "laying down one's life for a friend," but it was only through a personal and later-in-life experience that I realized how painfully ignorant I was about the meaning of this phrase. What I came to realize was that I had only associated the saying with Jesus's example on the cross and then those of martyrs and war heroes. For me laying down one's life meant being willing or choosing to die for someone or an important cause, and it was serious business. While not dwelling on the subject with any urgency in my youth and middle age, I knew that I didn't have what it would take to be that courageous.

Then later in life came a lesson. My husband had a major surgery and needed help with everything he did: sitting, standing, walking, bathing; getting in and out of—clothes, chairs, bed, braces, vehicles, home, church, stores. He couldn't lift or reach, twist or turn, lean or bend.

At first he didn't want to be a bother to me and I simply wanted to take good care of him. People were gracious in their offers to help, but we thought we could handle the situation without turning to or burdening others. For a while we stumbled through together, began figuring out a manageable routine. We'd smile when someone would say, "We'll be praying for both of you," grateful but without a clue what issues other than his healing might hold or entail a need for prayers for either of us.

While he was patient with the healing process, he wasn't always so patient with my timing or ways of doing things for him. I was trying to be patient with and meet his needs as best I could, but truth was, they interfered with my schedule, my routine, my comfort. We prayed a lot, together and separately, and had tremendous spiritual support from family, friends, our church and community, but it was only after a particularly hard afternoon that the revelation came. I was having a little pity party, grumbling to myself about how needy he was, how inconvenient illness is, how little time I had just for me anymore, and decided to take a walk. Not too far up the road thoughts began strolling in. I knew they were from the Holy Spirit because I immediately felt convicted:

> *You made a commitment to this man, to love, honor, and cherish through the best and the worst. What would you expect him to do if the roles were reversed? I know this is hard but you're always asking me to guide and lead you where I would have you go. You pray about being strengthened in your faith walk. You tell me you love Me and want to serve Me, but it seems you've forgotten what that means. I'm not asking you to die; I'm asking you to die to yourself because this isn't about you. I'm asking you to lay down your comfort, your routine, and what you want for a while and remember, "Greater love has no one than this: to lay down one's life for one's friend" (John 15:13). Caring for someone is perhaps the most important thing you can ever do for another human being.*

There it was. Jesus's Holy Spirit was asking me to lay down my insensitive thoughts, die to myself—my wants, my comfort, my selfish ways—turn to Him for help while serving another human being in need. By the time I finished my walk, tears had washed away all the anger and impatience and mean-spirited thoughts. My heart had been washed thoroughly by the conviction of the Holy Spirit. His was an offer to help in the situation by taking on my burdens and helping me realize what "laying down one's life" honestly and truly means at the mundane and daily level of living. As I stepped into the living room, I knew He'd been at work there, too, because my husband immediately apologized for being "short-tempered" with me and thanked me for all I was doing for him; he told me how much he appreciated my being here for him. We were reminded, *"You are My friends if you do what I command you. And this I command you, that you love one another"* (John 15:14, 17).

What I learned through this experience was that at home, hidden away from the spotlight of fellowship and the distraction of busyness, the way we treat our family members and neighbors is the best indicator as to how much we value the kindness, compassion, and love that the Lord has lavished on us (1 John 3:1). Being a caregiver can be demeaning at times, is definitely inconvenient, and can be frustrating, but if I cannot care for the disabled, sick, weak or disadvantaged in my own family, how can I say that I value God's love? Oh sure, it may cost time, energy, and self-sacrifice to care for someone else, but it cost God the life of His own Son to care for me (Romans 5:6–8).

It took this exacting lesson to help me realize what is most important in my life. I was learning and growing in my relationship with the Holy Spirit and with my husband, both of which are immeasurably encouraging and satisfying.

While now better able to focus on the subject with a newfound recognition and respect, I've come to trust and more fully know that I don't have the stuff it takes to be courageous or lay down my life for others except through relationship with Jesus, *"If we love one another, God abides in us, and His love is perfected in us"* (1 John 4:12). It has only been through the Holy Spirit's love working in me that I more fully came to understand what caregiving is all about in its entirety, and the truth is, it has already been summed up through the gospel of Jesus and His display of the greatest love there is—*laying down one's life for a friend.*

One Place I Can't Go

I love to go places,
whether in my mind
or actually down the road
to some place, any place,
and I love to go with you.

One place I can't go,
especially in my mind,
even on bright sunny days,
even when I'm not alone,
even at my bravest,
strongest,
most confident…

is the prospect and place
of going through life without you.

The Vitality of Living and Dying

Jesus said to her, *"I am the resurrection and the life;*
he who believes in Me will live even if he dies,
and everyone who lives and believes in Me
will never die. Do you believe this?"

—John 11:25–26

These Hands

These hands have braided
a thousand rugs
late at night after
all the chores are done,
all the family's asleep.

These hands have held
babies slick with afterbirth
and loved ones breathing
their last breath,
and then curled prayerful.

These hands have cooked
more than a thousand meals,
scrubbed pots and pans,
floors and walls, miles of sheets,
heads and ears dirty to clean.

These hands have warmed
and comforted, slapped
and stung, laid calmly in a lap
and bunched tight as they wrung
with worry for what's to come.

These hands have tended
and mended a lifetime of living
sewn honest and faithful
as they molded and folded,
always braiding with love.

If Looks Backward,
but Faith Looks Forward

"Life has meaning only in the struggle.
Triumph or defeat lies in the hands of God.
So let us celebrate the struggle."

—Swahili Warrior Song

While the day of his funeral was a sad and hard day, it was my hope
and intention that through a few words from Scripture and our presence as a community, we would offer comfort to a grieving family.
For Christians, death is not the end of life; however for this particular family and particular situation, the Swahili Warrior Song and
Ecclesiastes 3 seemed to encase what this young man's life had been
all about, so I used them to frame his service.

He had attended high school and was an all-star ball player and
athlete; he loved music and played both drums and guitar; he loved
the outdoors—especially, camping and fishing with his family, rock
hunting, and riding motorcycles. Black Mountain was a favorite
family spot where many of their happiest memories were generated.
Over the years came his times when he *built up, tore apart, embraced
and shunned embracing, laughed and danced, threw stones and gathered
stones, and experienced the birth of love* for the woman he chose to
give his heart, and the three best and most precious gifts in his life,
his children. These were the best and the worst of times, the most
important or central times of his life.

The family's biggest worry or fear was that others would choose to judge him and the times of his life, because seemingly, from an outside view, he did in fact choose to throw away and tear apart much of what he might have had or could have had. They knew all too well about his *times of war, his times of hell on earth.* However, I tried to stress how easily we all forget that none of us is alone in our walk; we are surrounded by, walking alongside family, friends, neighbors and co-workers, strangers and enemies alike. Everything we do is observed by and/or has an effect on others. Key to the point I tried to make is that none of us has any right to judge another. Scripture tells us clearly in Matthew 7:1–2: *"Do not judge so that you will not be judged. For in the way you judge, you will be judged; and by your standard of measure, it will be measured to you."*

The blessing in this young man's story came two years prior to his death, when he had finally reached a point; he realized his very life depended on his making better and different choices. Bottom line, he didn't want to die. He didn't want to leave his children and his family. He very much wanted to live and overcome and begin again. He admitted to those *times to let go* and was clinging to those *times to hold onto.* He had crawled up and through a time to hate and was clearly at *a time to give up as lost* that which he couldn't change, fix, or do anything about. He couldn't recover lost moments, days, or choices. Those were in the past. He needed to and wanted to move forward. He had a short *time to try to sew things together,* but it wasn't meant to be.

So we gathered that day in *a time to weep* and *a time to mourn.* My biggest worry was for the parents, siblings, children, and close friends. I heard a lot of guilt being expressed. So I said to them: true guilt, or sin, comes only as a result of breaking God's laws. However, when feelings of guilt arise when our conscience tells us we have simply failed to measure up to our own expectations or the standards other people have set for us—that's "false guilt." It usually comes from feelings of inadequacy—if only we'd have done more; if only he'd made better choices—if only things would have been better in his life, if only I'd have checked on him more often, if only the treatment would have worked, if only he'd have been strong enough for the transplant—*if only, if only, if only...*

Yes, there were times over the years when he wasn't following the ways that anyone would have wanted for his life, and certainly, his death was not the choice that anyone would have asked for him and was not how anyone wanted to say goodbye to him. I told the audience that I believe they, and indeed all of us must focus on God's grace each and every day, in all the circumstances of our lives. His was not an "only his story." It's the story of mankind in a fallen world.

I reminded them that *"if"* is a word that looks back on a past that cannot be changed. *If* raises a host of questions that only God can answer. *If* looks backward, but faith looks forward. I suggested that what we need is faith enough to believe in God's grace and control. With faith, *if* becomes our choice, our chance to follow *"His will be done on earth as it is in heaven"* or not. I prayed that God's truth and the hope that came with the resurrection of our Lord Jesus Christ would be or become the anchor that sustained this family and other families just like theirs through the days ahead. I prayed that they'd let go of guilt, begin to experience *a time of peace, a time of healing*, which hopefully might be followed by *a time to once again feel joy*, find renewed love and hope.

If the Swahili warrior song is true in that *"Life has meaning only in the struggle. Triumph or defeat lies in the hands of God,"* then yes, we struggle, sometimes really struggle, but life has meaning because through God and only through God can we overcome our struggles and know triumph. God's word from Romans 5:3–5 proclaims it true: *"we also exult in our tribulations, knowing that tribulation brings about perseverance; and perseverance, proven character; and proven character, hope, and hope does not disappoint, because the love for God has been poured out within our hearts through the Holy Spirit who was given to us."*

An Appointed Time for Everything: A Love Story

"There is an appointed time for everything.
And there is a time for every event under heaven."

—Ecclesiastes 3:1

Well-known author Mark Twain wrote, "Truth is stranger than fiction, but it is because fiction is obliged to stick to possibilities; truth isn't." And that was the genuineness of one of our most heart-wrenching love stories.

I'd known him for years; he and my husband had worked together on a construction project; then later, he spent some time in our hospice care with his father before he passed. It was through that time he came to know what hospice was all about and how we did business, so it didn't come as a surprise when a few years later and after receiving a terminal diagnosis, he called and said, "It's time." He checked himself in one weekend after a fall where he'd spent a few hours on the floor, unable to get up, unable to get to his phone and call for help.

In my role as chaplain, I met with him the following Monday, invited him to sit at the kitchen table so we could visit as I gathered information for the spiritual assessment. At one point, he excused himself, went to his room and came back with a picture of himself and a lovely fair-haired woman. His pensive expression foretold that this picture was telling a story. Even for someone who didn't know the circumstances, the picture captured the obvious—they were looking at one another through the eyes of love. He began, "This is my only regret in life."

They'd grown up together and dated in high school but she was a year older and moved on to college. He remained engrossed with finishing high school, his athletic endeavors, and being a typical teenager, while she got caught up in earning a degree and all that college life entailed. And so it went. Whether they had opportunity or attempted to reunite at any given time or not became a moot point.

After he graduated, he went to work, spent the majority of his life on the road, drove trucks, worked construction, forged ahead through four marriages. He chuckled with the telling, "Always looking for her in some way I suppose." Meanwhile, she earned her degree, went to work, married, widowed once and divorced once. Later, as they looked back, the most appropo saying that seemed to fit was Kipling's line from one of his ballads, "Never the twain shall meet," meaning, "Two things which are so different as to have no opportunity to unite."[3]

However, she believed that we should never discount what God has in store for us or the power of love. She quoted Ecclesiastes 3, *"There is an appointed time for everything. And there is a time for every event under heaven…"*

Once he learned he had cancer, he decided to do something about that one regret. He found out where she was living and called her. He found her in a "place" where she could and was willing—she flew in to meet and be with him for his first round of cancer treatment. Love reunited after forty odd years.

Responsibilities required that she return home. And so she did, but they talked daily, encouraged in their renewed love affair. He continued through the stages of his cancer, finally and only giving in after the doctors said the treatments weren't working. She flew back and forth to be at his side and spend time encouraging and loving him, treasuring the moments.

[3.] Rudyard Kipling from his Barrack-room ballads, 1892.

When apart, their hearts were broken, he'd fall into despair, question whether there was a God at all; he'd ask, "Why this? Why this way? Why now?" When together, nothing seemed impossible. Love gave him the courage to go on. Even when he became unable to talk, he'd rally every so often and let her know how grateful he was that she was by his side. She continued to thank God for this precious gift—this appointed time they had together. Yet she'd lose heart because home and responsibility would call her back. She talked about wrestling with her head versus her heart, "Should I stay? I don't want him to be alone." Theirs became a wrestling match of seemingly unbearable portions.

It's in 1 Corinthians 13:12–13, that we read and hopefully find an answer to any questions and any despair we may ever experience about love—that which we hold onto, that which we regret—all of which carry us through a lifetime. God informs us early on that we are not to know what He knows, *"For now we see in a mirror dimly, but then face to face; now I know in part, but then I will know fully just as I also have been fully known. But now faith, hope, love, abide these three; but the greatest of these is love."*

It wasn't meant for these two to know "Why this, why now, why this way?" It was only for them to be *"rooted and grounded in love... and to know the love of Christ which surpasses knowledge, that you may be filled up to all the fullness of God"* (Ephesians 3:17b, 19).

And that dear reader calls for a "No reservations, no retreats, no regrets type of love" because, *"Love never fails...bears all things, believes all things, hopes all things, endures all things"* (1 Corinthians 13:7). God set that up so that we might endure all things—*"times to give birth and times to die; times to tear down an times to build up; times to weep and times to laugh; times to embrace and times to shun embracing; times to tear apart and times to sew together; and a time for love and a time for peace"* (Ecclesiastes 3).

Because of her faith, she was able to eventually arrive at a good place regarding their love story. She chose to bear, believe, hope, and endure, quoting, "We do not love without gaining more than we could ever lose. We do not grieve without first knowing love."

As his condition worsened, volunteers or staff would call her and hold the phone up to his ear so she could talk to him. As his time neared, the nurse called and asked if she had any last words to say before he went. She said she gathered her thoughts and reassured him that she'd be okay, and that she'd love him to the stars and back forever. He died peacefully at his appointed time, wrapped in the arms of her love.

The Breath of Life

The hiss from his concentrator
whisks her back to when her mother
needed one to breathe and live.
Back then, the indicators of discomfort
were the furrowed lines on her forehead
and death grip on the arms of her chair
which belied the fact the machine helped
or eased her desperate fear that
without it, she'd die gasping for air
because always for her, each breath
came so laboriously hard.

Here now, he quietly implies his fear:
May have to hook up to it all the time—
not just at night, but permanently.
As his eyes close, she breathes a sigh
and finds solace in the rise and fall
of his chest as he draws in deeply.
He nods off as his head pillows
on the back of his recliner;
his hands rest lightly in his lap and
his face slackens as he softly sucks in
the gift of life, as he's finally
comfortable and able to breathe.

On Being Ready

"Therefore be on the alert, for you do not know which day your Lord is coming…for this reason you also must be ready; for the Son of Man is coming at an hour when you do not think He will."

—Matthew 24:42, 44

Despite her age, the months of her failing health, and eventually the doctor's diagnosis that she had but a few months to live, he did the same as so many of us tend to do—we choose not to think about death and dying, heaven or hell. Even though we have heard and or are somehow aware that, *"Even though I walk through the valley of the shadow of death"* (Psalm 23:4) we push it far away so that we don't have to look at it or give it any serious consideration. It hurts our hearts and frightens us to our very core; it leaves us confused and feeling helpless or lost, maybe hopeless. And so it was with him. He said they'd been married, and emphasized "happily," for fifty-three years. "She was my everything; took care of all of us, this house, the kids. Even me," he chuckled sardonically. "I don't know what I'm going to do without her." It was the same for all the weeks she was in our care. I would find him sitting outside on the back porch or off in an area all by himself with a hang-dog look on his face, timid and sad as a lost puppy. At different times I attempted to ferret out his thoughts about life and death: I asked what he liked to do in his spare time now that he was retired. "Be with her." I asked what hobbies he enjoyed as a young man; he shook his head, said he couldn't remember. I asked what plans they had made as a couple in the event of one of them passing before the other. None. I asked, "Have you given thought to her wishes regarding burial or cremation?" Nope. "Have you two ever talked about your wishes regarding your burial or cremation?" Nope. I asked about his faith system, what it had taught him regarding the very important eventuality, the fact that man is mortal and going to die. He was able to express that he believed in God but "maybe not so much today." He said he believed in heaven, but obviously couldn't see it while "stuck here in hell." If he had ever heard, *"God is to us a God of deliverances; and to God the Lord belong escapes from death"* (Psalm 68:20), he'd forgotten or given up on the words, the hope.

And so came the day, even when he *did not think it would.* His family gathered around, helped him make decisions, did all they could to ease his heartache. The sad truth was, there was no ease to his pain because he wasn't ready. The time had come but he had turned his ears from the Truth; he had walked in accordance to his own desires and plans without thought to what God's Word told him. He had chosen to ignore the gospel as recorded in 1 John 5:20–21, *"And we know that the Son of God has come, and has given us understanding so that we may know Him who is true; and we are in Him who is true, in His Son Jesus Christ. This is the true God and eternal life."* He had not guarded himself from the false idol of "If I don't think about it, it will go away." He was left with no defense.

Deeper In

(A Take on John 4:11–14)

After his death, the depth of her despair
seemed an endless, dry, and hollow well.
Her parched soul needed nourishment,
spoke of her spiritual condition
as she had nothing to draw from.
There was neither thought given to hope
nor belief held in faith for living water.

She had conformed to the ways of the world,
allowed herself to fall into the void,
but through the lovingkindness of God,
relief rose from a deep spring within.
The ache in her heart was transformed
by the renewing of her mind through
an allotted measure of faith in God.

So how did she find that living water?
It was the Holy Spirit who drew it up,
called her from the depths of her grief,
quenched her thirst for hope and the truth
when a friend shared, *"Everyone who drinks
of my water shall never thirst again
because it's a spring of eternal life."*

Jesus filled her up, satisfied her thirst
with: *"Come to Me, all who are weary
and heavy-laden, and I will give you rest."*
He wet her want with a word of hope
and she transformed by going deeper in.
The fountain of living water washed
the bitterness away with grace and love.

Such As It Is

She welcomed me into her home
with the comment, "Such as it is,"
and I assumed she meant how it looked.
As a woman, I understood—
we want guests to feel comfortable,
but as a stranger in this place,
I saw more than "such as it is."

As family came and wandered through,
the home came alive as love's poem
welcomed strangers, one and all
into the personal presence—
such as it was—such as they were,
which filled my soul as I observed
there was more to this just as it is.

Love radiated through her house
was gently affirmed by her ways.
From this woman and in her home
God's graciousness was magnified
as Grandmother spoke words of faith,
a hope and belief in His ways,
and lived for God—that's what it was.

In Her Mind

In her mind he's out a fencin'
or doin' chores around,
and he'll be in for dinner soon—
but only in her mind.

She stands and stares out the glass
from the home where she's been placed,
and ev'ry car's a horse and rider—
but only in her mind.

She's at the ranch, her family's here,
of this there is no doubt,
'cause she can see and hear them clear—
but only in her mind.

Her children play, the garden's growin'
and things are just the same;
she still bakes bread and works all day—
but only in her mind.

Flowers grow beneath the line
she planted there with care,
beside the house so tall and proud—
but only in her mind.

They moved her in a year ago,
she didn't cope with change;
nothing aged or ever died—
but only in her mind.

No, she doesn't feel the close confines
because she's at the ranch
with mem'ries strong and all in tact—
but only in her mind.

How Do You Want to be Remembered?

"You who know, O LORD, remember me, take notice of me..."

—Jeremiah 15:15

Through all the years and the numbers of people I've sat with who are in their final stage, or those who are caregiving for someone in the final stage of life, there's one truth that continually comes forward regardless of: their station in life; their race or gender; their hopes coming true or being dashed and forgotten; their faith or lack thereof; the length of their dying process; or the difficulty with or their acceptance of the dying process. One truth rose and continues to rise to the top—they all want to be remembered. I often ask, "How do you hope to be remembered?" These few captured replies are sincere, simple and complex, surprising and not, tender, thoughtful and thought-provoking.

> - "As a nice lady."
> - "As a hardworking man of integrity."
> - "That everyone I met knew that Jesus is!"
> - "I want to be remembered by my wife and children as a good husband and a good father. I want to be remembered as a man who held deep faith and even in the most inappropriate times, when I made mistakes, I knew and would do all I could to fix them."

➤ "That I was always happy and loved people. Happiness came as a combination of God's gift and my choice; I choose to forgive and forget; I don't let stuff that I can't fix or change get me down."

➤ "We were so blessed and our family had very few problems; we knew what we needed and wanted and supported one another through the process. I hope that my family remembers that I was always interested in learning—learning anything and everything about each of them. I cared about what they were doing and how they were doing; I was always in the middle of things and it helped keep me grounded, gave me purpose and intention."

➤ What is it in life that keeps us living and learning? There's so much beyond this world, these few miles, yet to know. It's why we must always be humble and kind and keep on keepin' on. I want people to remember me for that—I am always learning and as a result, I'm living.

A Tribute to a Dad

We recently saw a Father's Day segment about what an adult child had learned from his dad, so we decided we needed to put our thoughts down on paper about what we have learned from you:

- It pays to be patient and to think things through.
- You don't need to buy things on credit; wait until you have saved enough money to buy it.
- Don't eat yellow snow. (Never did try that one, so your guidance helped!)
- That a person can love deeply and completely, more than once.
- The school of hard knocks and hard labor is the best school of all.
- We can't go anywhere without somebody asking about you; a testament to how many lives you touched in the community.
- Picking rocks out of the yard builds character. Funny how this saying always came out right before you mowed the yard.
- Having an incredibly loyal friend who will walk with you every day is a great gift that not many get to experience.
- Money is only a tool and should be used that way.
- Bad jokes are only bad in the eyes of the beholder.
- Sacrificing for the family was never a sacrifice in your mind; it was a way of life.
- Family has a lot of different definitions.
- Acceptance of physical limitations doesn't mean weakness.

- Leadership is earned; it's not a title or a right.
- Keeping quiet is better than trying to argue. Especially if the argument is between two uncles.
- The thigh is the best part of the chicken.
- Heading to Boysen to fish with nothing but baloney sandwiches (or mustard sardines and Vienna sausages), poles, and bait is a pretty cool way to spend time with one of your kids.
- Throwing clubs on the golf course doesn't really accomplish as much as you think it will.
- That we have been blessed with a great dad, and not everybody gets that honor; so thanks for all your support, love, and understanding over the years.

Love you, Dad!

Companions of a Different Sort

"God saw all that He had made, and behold, it was very good."

—Genesis 1:31

There was purpose for it all—and I paraphrase loosely from Genesis 1—when God created the heavens and the earth, formed light from the darkness, named and separated the waters, which were below from the expanse which was above, called the dry land earth and let it sprout vegetation, brought forth living creatures of every kind, and lastly, created man in His own image, blessed him with dominion over all, and saw that it was good.

For this narrative's sake and as I have observed devotion and grief of all sorts, I suggest that while God brought forth a woman to be a companion to man, He also gave us friends of a different sort that we might find and enjoy a special comradeship in life. We are blessed to have volunteers in our community who train animals to be companions for those who are shut-in or ill; specifically, there are stories I will never forget which involved dogs.

I got the call from our nurse letting me know a female patient in the community was actively dying and the family was asking for spiritual support. When I arrived, a large and beautiful golden retriever met me at the door. A family member came quickly, apologizing for her, and promptly escorted her to the back porch. I joined the family in the bedroom and anointed and prayed over the woman, and after she passed, we moved to the living room where we gathered in a family circle. Someone opened the patio doors and the golden retriever quietly threaded her way through us and went straight to the bedroom.

The wailing began. We found the retriever with her head lying on the still body, emitting a low moaning that was one of the most mournful shows of grief I'd ever heard. She remained in that position, her cry continuing even while and after they moved her out back again so the nurse and CNA could prepare the body. The family reported that she returned to the bedroom for days afterward, obviously missing and grieving the loss of her friend.

Another time, I got the call that a community patient was actively dying but by the time I got to the home, he had passed. His favorite companion, a gentleman Dachshund was lying on his master's lap and had been throughout the morning and dying process. When the nurse and funeral director attempted to pick the dog up so they could prepare the body, they had to literally peel the dog off his master. He stretched out full body, holding physical contact until the very last second. A family member had to take him outdoors for a walk because he simply wouldn't be distracted from getting back up in the chair. They said he sighed and cried as only a dog can for days afterward.

Yes, disease is insidious, and death comes "like a thief in the night" but neither disease nor death can clear love from the heart of one of God's creatures. With an everlasting lovingkindness, God promises He will have compassion for us. He's the One who brought forth living creatures of every kind and gave the one He created in His own image dominion over all and called it good. We were meant for love and to be loved. What a blessing to have another of God's creatures remind us of this truth.

The Hardest Part

She said the hardest part of dying wasn't hearing the diagnosis—she'd known something wasn't right in her body for a while. It wasn't about leaving her family behind, except she admitted that was going to be hard, and she hadn't yet decided what to and what not to share with them. Said she couldn't even begin to think about the many celebrations and events she would miss with grandkids and great grands. And it wasn't about where she was going. She had believed in and trusted God since childhood. She believed there was a heaven, and that by trusting in Jesus she would be accepted into His kingdom. No, for her, the hardest part came before and was in the form of the slow-arriving realization which came like a sudden punch in the gut but was the unanticipated truth: "I'm old," she said, "and I don't know when it started exactly or how it got here so darned quick." She shook her head in wonderment.

As time passed, she spent her last weeks in reflection; said it all began around age seventy, when seemingly everything began to change—the subtle and the obvious. While she recognized and celebrated that in many ways she was much smarter about life, much more accepting of others and who she was: a woman who had grown in her confidence and ability to make wise decisions with both feet on solid ground. Then, as if overnight, she found she couldn't remember where she laid her glasses. Even found them on top of her head once after she had searched her home and car from top to bottom. She said she'd get ready to introduce a long-time friend and couldn't remember his/her name. The new, young receptionist at the bank wouldn't let her make a withdrawal one day because she couldn't remember her account number—the one she'd had for forty years. Found a carton of sour cream in the pantry that she'd bought two days before, found the can of beans in the refrigerator.

She supposed she'd simply chosen to not think about all the aches and pains and tendencies to leak—from her eyes, nose, and crotch;,said "Once it starts, I can't stop it. No keigel." She felt at times like her body was betraying her, and it ticked her off, admitted she began to recognize that she got tired more quickly, didn't have the same energy level she had in the pas and couldn't do some of the physical or mental things she used to do so easily. She became frustrated when trying to accomplish something and finding there was a limit to what she could do. She had the added issue of having to watch her spouse age and experience his own health issues and eventual death. She remembered days when they thought they could conquer the world and a minor headache was their only health issue. Time began to move too fast, things got harder/more complicated and took longer and seemed tougher. She emphasized, "It just doesn't seem fair," but she remembered her grandmother warning her, "Just you wait and see."

For her, the watershed came the summer she began falling. Turned around in the yard to move a hose and fell flat on her side. No rock, stump, lump, or bump. The first time nothing was hurt, "except my pride." The most embarrassing came a few weeks later when she stopped alongside a dirt road to relieve herself. Had done it a hundred times over the years with no problem. That day, as she squatted by the driver's seat, the wind blew the door into her behind. Knocked her down to her knees, twisted her ankle in an awkward position that "hurt like the dickens." Her bladder emptied quickly— all over panties and capris and new sandals. She was mortified. Alternated between laughing at the thought of someone watching from afar and crying because she just couldn't figure out why this was happening to her all of a sudden. Swore she wouldn't tell a soul, "Until now."

That day, she asked, "How am I going to get up from this, Lord?" It was at that moment she said she knew her prayer wasn't about just getting up from an awkward or embarrassing physical position but from the difficult to maneuver through, unlooked-for, put off truth and fact that she was facing the end of her life—maybe not the month or year, but certainly was in the latter stage of life as she had always known and experienced it. It was a defining moment as she drove down the back roads to get herself home—with a whole lot of metaphor applicable to the situation in which she found herself.

Afterward, it took her a while—many agonizing, thoughtful, and prayerful hours in contemplation as she began to look the situation "square in the eye." She knew it was a trust issue and turned to Scripture: "In God I have put my trust, I shall not be afraid" (Psalm 56:11a). "Indeed, we have the sentence of death within ourselves so that we will not trust in ourselves, but in God who raises the dead; delivers us from so great a peril of death, and will deliver us, He on whom we have set our hope" (2 Corinthians 1:9–10). And finally, the one that gave her the most reassurance and peace she sought:

Psalm 23

The LORD is my shepherd,
I shall not want.
He makes me lie down in green pastures;
He leads me beside still waters.
He restores my soul;
He guides me in the paths of righteousness
For His name's sake.

Even though I walk through the valley of the
shadow of death,
I fear no evil, for You are with me;

You prepare a table before me in the presence of
    my enemies;
You have anointed my head with oil;
My cup overflows.
Surely goodness and lovingkindness will follow
    me all the days of my life,
And I will dwell in the house of the LORD
    forever.

At Whose Table Do We Sit?

A Study of Ecclesiastes

Oh, woe-is-me, life-is-meaningless
Ecclesiastes has nothing over his sister.
Bitterness is an old hag sitting
at the table of life, hateful hanging
out the corner of her disgruntlement.
"Life's a bitch, and then you die,"
she hacks out like so much phlegm.

The whole family's been infected
and can't rise above the monotony:
twin sister, Regret, sprawls at the table,
feeds her resentment with the meat
of should'a, could'a, and if only.
Brother Guilt doesn't say much,
just stands at the stove,
occasionally stirring the pot.

Dissatisfied cousins join the meal:
Unworthiness sets the table by placing
excuses like napkins at each chair.
Brokenness drops the platter of promises while
Sorrow slumps in the corner,
unaware of anyone else in the room.
Shame hides in the basement,
snivels, "I'll be up after a while."

They seemingly wait expectantly,
when predictably, Anger arrives,
tromps in, takes a seat at the head.
Pity steals in, tries to soothe the scene
but her pathetic mews are overwhelmed
as Futility is served by the maid, Defeat,
who later leaves Lonely to clean up the mess.

Consumed by their labors under the sun,
they are blinded by Adversity's darkness
and miss the one ray of Life in the room—
pictured on the wall is God's gift to man—
a revealing of eternity at the table of
Jesus Christ in accord with his followers:
"For whoever is joined with all the living, there is hope."

Looking Death in the Eye:
A Step-by-Step Process

"Indeed, we had the sentence of death within ourselves so that we would not trust in ourselves, but in God who raises the dead; who delivered us from so great a peril of death, and will deliver us, He on whom we have set our hope."

—2 Corinthians 1:9–10

I am often blessed by special times of reconciliation with a patient in the dying process, but none were as extraordinary as hers. As a medical professional, she knew too much about her disease and its progression. When I suggested that her insights into the dying process might be invaluable to others, she began talking; talking like she hadn't with me or perhaps anyone, but most critically and especially with herself. She astutely assessed the time as "looking death square in the eye."

It was a step-by-step process. She began the telling by going back several years. She told about being with an uncle while he was dying from chronic obstructive pulmonary disease (COPD) and saying to herself, *"This is how I'm going to die someday."* The revealing brought tears to her eyes, and she said she acknowledged it way back then, but it still wasn't enough to stop her from smoking. As a result, she felt guilty of denying God's best for her.

Step 1: *"I **acknowledged** my sin to You, and my iniquity I did not hide; I confessed my transgressions to the Lord, and You forgave the guilt of my sin."* (Psalm 32:5)

Years later, she said the realization—the acceptance that smoking was hindering her abilities—was the hardest of all: thinking about having to quit her job; leave the people and the work she loved; stop doing the very thing that most joyfully and purposefully fed her soul, filled her heart to full. A professional person, she loved her career, *"Enjoyed it all,"* but began realizing that she could no longer be as efficient as she wanted to be. She agonized over the decision of doing what was best and right after noticing that she was not as quick in her thoughts and reactions as she needed to be. She said she was able make the decision to stop working based on a commitment she had made at the beginning of her career—she promised herself she'd only work as long as she could serve people and their well-being competently.

Step 2: *"And those are the ones on whom seed was sown on the good soil; and they hear the word and accept it and bear fruit, thirty, sixty, and a hundredfold."* (Mark 4:20)

I was there the week she decided to make the move from her home to the hospice facility.

The slow process of living isolated after years of working with the public on a daily basis had taken its toll. It was after she found herself talking to the dog, telling him he'd have to wait a minute because she couldn't get up out of her chair to let him out. It became more apparent when she had to ask for help planting her garden and flowers because she simply didn't have the energy. Even though the doctor couldn't answer, "How long?" It was these "can't do anymores" that made her painfully but decisively aware that she was in the end stages of a lung ailment.

Step 3: *"**Submit** therefore to God…humble yourselves in the presence of the Lord, and He will exalt you."* (James 4:7, 10)

She was taken to the point at which she could not fall back on any intellectual, physical, or emotional human resource; her only hope was to trust in God's power to deliver her, a Christian chosen by Him for salvation, through a God who she believed would stand with her and keep His promise to neither leave nor forsake her.

Step 4: *"In God I have put my **trust**, I shall not be afraid…for You have delivered my soul from death, indeed my feet from stumbling, so that I may walk before God in the light of the living."* (Psalm 56:11–13)

Slowly but surely she began taking care of everything that she could control or fix, those she felt were important and/or necessary. She said, *"I wanted to get everything cleaned up and taken care of so there was nothing left undone."* She talked with family and designated those she deemed able to make choices for her; she met with the social worker and set up all the legal documents; she did all she could to help her son resolve some issues; she contacted the funeral home and made those arrangements, and through it all, she was unpretentiously reconciling herself to the fact that she was indeed dying.

On the anniversary of being in the hospice home a year, she smiled when she said, *"I didn't expect to be here this long."* The truth was, she had spent the entire year resolving issues, dealing with concerns, taking care of business so that others wouldn't be burdened with her "stuff." Even though she went through all this process, she never lost sight of her greatest earthly gift from God—her compassion. She would scold members of our staff and volunteers for not taking care of themselves, and she was endless in her sharing and caring for all the rest of us. Her truest and greatest gift of all was her love for others. Whether she realized it or not, she was still serving people and their well-being competently. It had indeed been a year of reckoning. It would seem that once a caregiver, always a caregiver, and she was one who walked before God in the light of the living.

Panning for Gold

*"He will sit as a smelter and purifier of silver, and He will purify
the sons of Levi and refine them like gold and silver,
so that they may present to the LORD offerings in righteousness."*

—Malachi 3:3

As I sat and visited with members of his family, I learned that panning for gold was one of his hobbies, a favorite pastime, and it was
those three words—*panning for gold*—that kept repeating themselves
in my mind. Leaning heavy on the metaphor and with that as a reference point, what I came to understand about this man was, it was
a term that applied across the board in his life.

First and foremost, he was a man of God. Neither he nor his
family claimed he was a churchgoing man, or a strict, religious man;
he was a believer in Jesus Christ's saving grace, chose to accept the
offer of forgiveness with a repentant heart, and believed in the hope
of eternal life with God. He was a faithful student of the Bible. Psalm
106:3 was his, *"Blessed are those who keep justice, and he who does righteousness at all times."* I dared to suggest that God was panning for
gold when he gave life to this particular individual.

However, panning for gold requires careful attention to and
study of the geology and lay of the land and then a whole lot of seeking and straining. God's work in each of us might be referred to as
panning for the gold. For example, His Word tells us in Deuteronomy
4:27–29, *"The LORD will scatter you among the peoples, and you will*

be left few in number among the nations...But from there you will seek the LORD your God, and you will find Him if you search for Him with all your heart and all your soul." Proverbs 8:17 reaffirms and reassures us all, *"I love those who love me; and those who diligently seek me will find me."*

In the sifting or sieving of life, this man consistently rose to the top. Family spoke of countless hours visiting with him by phone on the many issues they had in common. He was loving and compassionate and knowledgeable on many topics. He always asked about each member of any family and closed each conversation with an "I love you."

His wife believed there was a divine hand at work in the arrangement of their marriage. She said when she was thirteen years old she told her sister, "I'm going to marry him some day." It took her until she was twenty to accomplish that, but she was able to tell him before he died that even if she lived another 150 years, he would still be the only man for her. While she admitted that the years weren't all easy and wonderful, she wouldn't trade one of them. They were devoted to one another for fifty-eight years. I reiterate: it takes time, work, and some heat to purify gold.

According to his sons, he was a teacher, a patient, kind, loving, level-headed, trustworthy, talented man of his word. He was a friend and the kind of man who took pride in his family and his work. He taught much about life. One son remembered at about age thirteen, he decided to run away. He got about half a mile away from home when his dad drove up and asked, "So you're gonna run away?" When the son nodded, his dad simply said, "Well, why don't you give me a minute to pack and I'll run away with you." There was no recrimination, no anger, just love, patience, and understanding. Today, that son credits his dad with saving his life as he came to understand that his dad found a way to keep him busy, give him something meaningful to do, a purpose in life. There's that metaphor panning for gold again.

Finally and most importantly, as a man of God, he was ready. After his wife and son on separate occasions found the courage to reassure him that they would be okay and that he could and should go when he was ready, the son noticed his father looking past him, looking out to the patio doors, and then he raised his hand, as if waving someone to come in. His dad's focus at that point was on where he was going, and they believe an angel came to escort him home. You see, he was ready; he wasn't afraid. All the silt and sludge had been sifted away, the refining was done. Jesus was welcoming him home. And for this family, they believe their husband and father finally hit it rich; however instead of panning for, he would forever-more be gazing at streets of gold.

Job 22:25 speaks it well: *"Then the Almighty will be your gold and choice silver to you."*

A Time to Weep and
a Time to Laugh

Ecclesiastes 3

I always enjoyed going into their home because theirs was a love apparent, one built on trust in God and one another. Plus, they made the conscious decision to keep laughter and joy at the forefront. He told me more than once, "Even if you are dying, you still have to find ways to laugh." And amid their time of weeping, this hospice patient and his wife and caregiver found ways to laugh.

Toward the end of his disease progression, he'd often find himself lying in his bed, unable to stand on his own anymore, needing assistance to get from his wheelchair to his bed, to the shower, to the table. He became unable to complete simple daily tasks we too often take for granted, so he chose to move to the hospice home. I'd be telling a fib if I said he handled it all graciously every day. However, once he finally determined he was nearing the end of his life, his choice was as Paul wrote in Hebrews 2:13, *"I will put my trust in Him."* He turned it all over to God—his worries, his fears, his frustration, his anger, his sadness. That choice made the difference and helped them both maintain a quick wit through it all because they chose to find the humor in every situation.

While he had lost his physical ability to move around, he had not lost mental capabilities, especially his ability to flirt. And flirt he did with everyone, including the chaplain. On one particularly hard day the nurse had called me in because he was struggling emotion-ally. I found him alone, lying in bed, staring out the window. I knelt by his bed and together we began to sort through what was weighing so heavy on his heart. After a good long talk about this, that, and the other, we ended our time together in prayer, and that's when his wife walked in the room.

She quietly commented that she'd seen we were in a serious conversation so had gone to the kitchen to have coffee with some of the others at the hospice home. However, she then placed one hand on her hip and gave her husband a serious look and in a louder voice said, "I saw you in here holding hands and flirting with the minister, honey."

Despite his previous melancholy, and without missing a beat, he quickly replied, "Well, did you see that I had her on her knees right here, babe," as he pointed to the floor right beside his bed. Laughter erupted from deep within both their hearts and carried out and down the hall, proving it truly is the best medicine.

Later as we sat together at the dining room table, they began reminiscing about their many years of marriage. At one point he looked into her eyes and quoted a song saying, "When I think about love, I think of you." All joking aside, his sincerity brought tears to all listeners' eyes. We were at once reminded: *there is an appointed time for everything, every event under heaven—a time to weep and a time to laugh...*a time to embrace, a time to keep, a time to speak, and a time to love. And it was from their trust in God that they had found a way to let the peace of Christ rule in their hearts by embracing laughter and love.

It Takes Time to Forgive

"Do not remember the iniquities of our forefathers against us;
let Your compassion come quickly to meet us, for we are brought
very low. Help us, O God of our salvation, for the glory of
Your name; and deliver us and forgive our sins for Your name's sake."

—Psalm 79:8–9

How one's lifespan is handed out affects the whole of an outlook or attitude. All that we experience becomes our reality; it's all we know and so becomes the truth for us. It was hard for her to help us comprehend, but we simply couldn't imagine what she'd been through. When born during a time of war, there can be no easy explanation or clear understanding. Her anger would rise up when she'd try to express the reality of what she had undergone, so we often heard the hatred, tasted her bitterness, observed the stinging blows of years of unforgiveness as it pertained to her emotional and spiritual well-being.

However, her closest friends were able to describe how she attempted to overcome those feelings by "seeing the beauty around her." While he was still alive, she and her husband found solace in one another, traveled—loved to explore beautiful mountain ranges, and listened to lovely music together. They eventually found their way to the Wind River Range of Wyoming, where in addition, she took up gardening and enjoyed friendship with cats.

During her ninety-three years of living, she developed a list of theories about life in general:

1. Don't be a dope and work all the time. In the end bosses don't always appreciate it and many will take advantage of you.
2. Don't be fooled. I grew up in a time of propaganda and I recognize it here, now.
3. Go home, rest, take care of yourself and your family.
4. Cats are better than dogs!
5. War is ultimately about pride, power, and money, and it's the hardworking man and his family who suffers most. What a waste—the death of all those young men.
6. Read, educate yourself, don't believe everything you're told.
7. How do we really know? It takes faith.

She taught us that forgiveness is hard-earned, ambiguous, and may take years to attain. From her story we learned that while it's easy to say, *I forgive*, pardoning someone or some past and long-standing hurt is not so easy to carry out. In her case, she had harbored a hurt, fear, and anger for most of her life. However, it was through her story—especially the living it out to the end—that we learned while forgiveness doesn't come easy to mankind, it [pardon/forgiveness] is who and what our most gracious God is all about. She demonstrated grudgingly, in the very last of her days, that His mercy is patient, *"But You are a God of forgiveness, gracious and compassionate, slow to anger and abounding in lovingkindness; and You did not forsake [me]"* (Nehemiah 9:17b).

And it was her belief in God, not religion, but her faith that there was a God that she could pray to, that carried her through. It was our final prayer that she'd gotten to a place of forgiveness in her heart, that she knew His peace in the end, *"For this reason I say to you, her sins, which are many, have been forgiven, for she loved much...And He said to the woman, 'Your faith has saved you; go in peace'"* (Luke 7:47–50).

A Spirit of Rejection

"For the Lord searches all hearts, and understands every intent of the thoughts. If you seek Him, He will let you find Him; but if you forsake Him, He will reject you forever."

—1 Chronicles 28:9

When I was young, the naive in me wanted to believe that because everyone was born of God they therefore were inherently good and would be saved. I denied there was evil in the world because I didn't like to think about it, and argued that we come from God and He is good. I chose to forget the part about the "fall" and managed to walk through many years regarding things from behind a pair of "rose-colored glasses"; that is until the day I walked into room 3.

She was lying in bed, propped up slightly, pale and frail under the covers. Initially she smiled, welcomed me to her bedside, but when I identified myself as the Chaplain, the physical response changed. While impossible, she seemed to shrink back into the mattress as tears welled up, brow furrowed, head began shaking side to side. Concern swept through me. It was instantly and obviously apparent something was wrong, so I began backing away, attempted to reassure her by saying that I didn't mean to upset her, that I'd come by at a better time. Her lip quivered, her eyes rolled up, saliva foamed out the corner of her mouth.

I moved out into the hall, called to the nurse, then leaned up against the wall, concern and tears welling up. I'd never experienced a response like that before and in the confusion, took it personally.

As it turned out, she wasn't in the throes of dying that first visit. I didn't attempt another visit for a few days, but staff and family reported that she was adjusting to the hospice setting, was able to sit up in her chair and visit a little. I decided to try again. I began by asking God's help on how to best approach this woman before I walked into the room. I decided it would be best to introduce myself as a volunteer, see if that made her less uncomfortable. But not to be. I didn't even get halfway into the room; the response was immediate—her physical being pulled back from me before I spoke a word. It was me—my presence, my voice, my looks—something about my presence was offensive to her. I backed toward the door once again, apologizing as tears began to roll down her cheeks. It was frightening and confusing for both of us. I moved out into the hall where my own tears began flowing.

This time, however, a granddaughter was there. She apologized for her grandmother's "reaction," explaining that years before there had been an incident with a minister. Her grandmother had never forgotten the event nor forgiven him. It evidently had been so horrific that this once woman of faith had given up on God, was still mad at Him, could not forget nor would she forgive what God had—in her opinion—let happen to her.

The anxiety, anger, and anguish carried through to the end. Family members tried talking to her, worried over her, prayed for her. Other staff attempted to help the woman reconcile her feelings so that she might have peace of mind, some hope restored. Nothing doing. Because of her emotional and spiritual dis-ease, she suffered to the end. I believe she, and those who were with her at the time observed a glimpse of hell on earth through her dying process.

I tell this story with an everlasting sadness. All that the spiritual portion of hospice care stands for—comfort and peace through forgiveness and hope—was rejected by this woman.

Jesus spoke of rejection in John 12:48: *"He who rejects Me and does not receive My sayings, has one who judges him; the word I spoke is what will judge him at the last day.*" It's a situation and human being whom I'll never forget. It was the first time I met with a spirit of rejection because of who I am in Christ.

I still wrestle with the sadness, the futility, wondering if I could have done something differently to help her; it didn't have to be that way, but God's word is clear: *"Do not grieve the Holy Spirit of God, by whom you were sealed for the day of redemption. Let all bitterness and wrath and anger and clamor and slander be put away from you, along with all malice. Be kind to one another, tender-hearted, forgiving each other, just as God in Christ also has forgiven you"* (Ephesians 4:31–32).

Needless to say, I no longer walk around hiding behind rose-colored glasses.

Reaching Back

She reaches back for words
to explain herself today,
but once again, recall fails her.
I sit, smile and nod, hesitant
to try and help her because
she's eager to share her thoughts.

The present seems mostly gone
so she reaches back to what once was
a place and time familiar and hers,
but only finds bits and pieces—
the rest is lost for today.

She's encouraged by my presence,
so she chatters her scattered thoughts,
reaches back and back,
grasps at wisps of memories
and shares them as best she can.

"When is Sissy coming?"

was his copyrighted question.

She was his escape hatch—
way out of the unfamiliar maze—
his life line; Sissy, the only one
he remembered with any clarity—
her, a border collie, and his sheep.

Alzheimer's is insidious:
fleeces memory empty,
flushes time and connections.

A busy ranch woman, Sissy
was unable to come visit often,
cried all the way home when she did.
He wept silently through the haze,
mind wrangling to recall anything
as he wandered and wondered where he was.

Alzheimer's is insidious:
clears memory of clarity,
rapes recognition raw.

Rare were the happy days when we
calmed him by talking about the ranch.
He remembered times below zero
when the truck wouldn't start,
or lambing, busiest time of the year.
He knew she needed to be home.

Alzheimer's is insidious:
robs reason gone,
deals dignity done.

But in those rare times of recollection,
like when Alice brought in the collie,
we saw his old self resurrect as he
leaned down, petted her, began talking
words we hadn't heard from him in months—
on the ranch, with his dog, working sheep.

Alzheimer's is insidious,
but even it can't clear
love from the heart of a soul.

Finding God: A Love Affair with Life

"Actually, I don't have a sense of needing anything personally.
I've learned by now to be quite content whatever my circumstances."

—Philippians 4:11

A former US Senator named Frank Carlson wrote: "God is looking for men. He wants those who can unite together around a common faith, who can join hands in a common task, and who have come to the kingdom for such a time as this. God give us men."[4] What God wants and what this world so desperately needs is literally why man is here on earth, and figuratively it represents the struggle of living. It's why God breathed life into a man: in whom the courage of God Everlasting ran still, deep, and strong; who was not for sale; who knew his place and filled it; who stood for what was right and told the truth; and looked the world square in the eye.

That's what we were gathered to celebrate the day of his funeral—a life lived well and full.

He wrote and/or organized much of his service around music and his philosophy on life and titled it, "A Love Affair with Life." He told me, "As I listen to music, I'm often caught up in a catchy tune: sometimes the rhythm, the drum beat, a special instrument, and often the lyrics express my feelings and thoughts." The first song

---

4. "What is the World Looking For?" From the late US Senator, Frank Carlson.

he chose expressed his belief and represented the very adhesive that sustained life for him. He asked a close friend to sing it. "The Love of God" is a melody that expressed the root and the source of his enduring, unwavering faith.

He summed up his life in three words—a love affair—the good and the bad, the happy and sad, the confrontations and the obstacles. His one big sadness was that he didn't recognize that truth until a later age, and it's that which was most tender and weighed heavy on his heart. He wished he'd been more aware earlier. He said things would have been easier for his wife. We talked about guilt versus regret. Contrary to what he feared or ignored, the simple truth was he was human and made mistakes. However, I believe he got to a place of acceptance that his life had been all it was meant to be.

During our conversations, he expressed the love affair he enjoyed with God, which was the precursor, the foundation and basis for the rest of his life. Second only to the love affair he treasured with God, was the one he had with his wife and family, which was based most fondly and wholly on the love affair he had with and because of the loving care of his mate. He said, "Something like sixty-six years ago, my heart was stopped by a beautiful person. After that many years, including many struggles, hard times and good times, defeats, and successes, and climbing hills together, her unconditional love is still stopping my heart." He said much of his contentment in life came from her support, and a major part of their love affair with life was that they both tried to give back. He said they both loved kids and teaching. Later, they enjoyed owning their own business. Their years of traveling brought them much satisfaction, introduced them to many wonderful people, and they enjoyed every moment of each and every experience. For him it all spelled contentment.

Scripture has plenty to say about contentment, but he was especially fond of Philippians 4:7–13; the Message's interpretation was his favorite: *"Before you know it, a sense of God's wholeness, everything coming together for good, will come and settle you down. It's wonderful what happens when Christ displaces worry at the center of your life. 8 Summing it all up, friends, I'd say you'll do best by filling your minds and meditating on things true, noble, reputable, authentic, compelling, gracious—the best, not the worst; the beautiful, not the ugly; things to praise, not things to curse. Put into practice what you learned from me, what you heard and saw and realized. Do that, and God, who makes everything work together, will work you into his most excellent harmonies. I'm glad in God, far happier than you would ever guess—happy that you're again showing such strong concern for me. Not that you ever quit praying and thinking about me. You just had no chance to show it. Actually, I don't have a sense of needing anything personally. I've learned by now to be quite content whatever my circumstances. I'm just as happy with little as with much, with much as with little. I've found the recipe for being happy whether full or hungry, hands full or hands empty. Whatever I have, wherever I am, I can make it through anything in the One who makes me who I am."*

He had come to know full well that real contentment is not automatic, it must be learned over time, and second, it only comes through the supernatural love of Christ—"through Him who strengthens me."

He continued: "As my time here on earth comes to an end, I feel a need to share my thoughts and feelings with loved ones. It is my desire to humbly convey them to my devoted wife, my beloved children and their families, and to many dear and cherished friends. Each of you have given me something special and enriched my life in so many positive ways. Life is filled with hills and valleys. There are many obstacles and sad times. I have found confronting such challenges with positive thoughts and actions pays desired dividends."

He spent the last few months of his life planning and organizing (we called it frettin' and stewin' about) the service, trying to take care of business so that his family didn't have anything to worry about or deal with after he left. You see, once a husband, always a husband; once a father, always a father; once a teacher, always a teacher.

He had another friend sing, "Love is a Many Splendored Thing." Then he asked me to read the words I'd read and spoken over him when I anointed him the night before he died—The Twenty-Third Psalm. He said, "I want that." I took that to mean, he wanted me to share that it was his hope to lie down in green pastures, walk beside still waters, be restored in his soul and led in the path of righteousness, where goodness and mercy would follow him all the days of his life, that he might dwell in the house of the LORD forever. That was his heart and hope.

He most wanted everyone—family and friends alike—to experience, to come to have a sense of God's wholeness that he'd experienced; he said: "It's wonderful what happens when Christ displaces worry at the center of your life." He wanted others "to do your best by filling your minds and meditating on things true, noble, reputable, authentic, compelling, gracious—the best, not the worst; the beautiful, not the ugly; things to praise, not things to curse." He prayed we would, "Put into practice what you learn, what you hear and see and realize...that God, who makes everything work together, will work you into his most excellent harmonies." He wanted all to be "glad in God, far happier than you would ever guess and to be happy with little as with much." He found the recipe for being happy had nothing to do with stuff or whether he was full or hungry or his hands were full or empty. He came to know, "I can make it through anything in the One who makes me who I am." In other words, he wanted every one of his family and friends to have a love affair with Jesus Christ.

This father and grandfather attempted to bring strength and stability to a family and a feeling of security to life. He taught by example a sense of values and self-worth and a foundation of love to last a lifetime. And it's for those things: the guidance and trust, solid advice and labors of love, for each sacrifice and the forgiveness that came without a second thought for anything and everything, that a man is loved and admired so much. He demonstrated wisdom, courage, and strength. He gave his time. His family gave him love, and that's all he said he ever needed or asked for.

I Searched for God

I saw evidence of God in the vastness of the universe,
In the beauty of the mountains and plains,
In all the earth and inhabitants.
I saw evidence of God in my fellow man.
I saw evidence of God in church.
I discovered God dwelt within myself, and
He required from me: faith humility, compassion, service, and love.
In return, He gave enduring love peace, and contentment.
I found God.[5]

[5.] "I Searched for God" by Jim Eager.

The Ordinary Sacred

"Therefore, my brothers, be all the more eager to make your calling and election sure, for if you do these things, you will never fall, and you will receive a rich welcome into the eternal kingdom of our Lord and Savior Jesus Christ."

—2 Peter 1:10–11

The man was always smiling, offering a warm handshake, and was gracious and friendly, even with a terminal diagnosis. It was a privilege to spend time with him because we had favorite pastimes, teaching, and our faith in common. We talked books, education, students, Christianity, and life—well, actually, he talked, and I mostly listened. But those were precious times for me because it seemed he was proving an old saying about choosing to die the same way he lived—right up to the last with great energy and courage. At one point in his last hours, one of our nurses was giving him some pain medication and she warned him, "This might make you kinda dopey." Without missing a beat, he said, "I never could keep those seven dwarfs straight; now who are they again?" As she named them off, he held up a finger for every one and said, "Yeah, yeah, it was Dopey I could never remember."

It was that sense of humor, that ability to very much be in and respectful of *the ordinary, sacred moments of life* that drew others in. At his funeral, I attempted to capture and share sacred moments from his ordinary story that best defined him through the veil of memories.

Though perhaps he would never have thought about his life in this way, his was a symbol of the hard-won success he achieved in his rise from a simple farm boy background to those of athlete, husband, father, teacher, coach, carpenter, pianist, artist, historian, and proud head of a family.

I could have stopped right there and said enough, summed up this man's life with a couple of preordained, God-designed words: *faithful leader*. However, there was more to this man's story because he chose to be a coach in life and to the last moment.

He and his wife were an ordinary couple raising what they claimed was an extraordinary family. They savored their ordinary times and chose to do so with great joy—intentionally practiced and perfectly executed. The truth was, woven in were also the times of tearing down and throwing away and shunning and wanting to give up as lost and throwing away. There were those times to tear apart, times to be silent and times to speak. But it was *the ordinary sacred*[6]—a phrase I'd love to take credit for but is a Kent Nerburn quote and title of one of his books—that I used to define this man's walk.

In this book, Nerburn wrote: "The truest measure of our hearts is how well we create love and hope in the hearts of children," and I added to that, all those with whom we come in contact, especially our family. Through his life and death, I was reminded of the measure of this man, as God intended him to be, that even though there were those rocky times, he always believed that it would be better; he trusted God and respected his wedding vows. His wife said, "We were better together than apart." He wasn't a man to put on airs, and while not one to say 'I love you' all the time, was quite sentimental. And she said that even though his diagnosis was never conclusive, "He accepted it as it came. We'd run back and forth to doctor's appointments, and he'd never complain. He didn't like being stuck in the house, in bed so much of the time, but you wouldn't know it. He was very courageous."

[6.] Ordinary Sacred by Kent Nerburn.

The family agreed that he was complex and simple all rolled into one. They also used the words: fighter, highly intelligent, creative, articulate, stubborn, and passionate. He chose to live a meaningful life; mediocrity was not part of his vocabulary. And despite being well educated and highly intelligent, he was quite humble and would often say, "I'm not very smart about things," or "I don't know much, but what I do know is…" A son agreed with the humble part by saying, "Dad often sold himself short. His attention to detail drove us crazy but was most endearing." They believe that the measure of their dad in most respects was the fact that he was always fair, "the most unbiased person in the world."

He was a man of conviction, a man of honor, a man of character, and he held expectations in that regard; he liked and respected people of character; he respected forthrightness. He handed discipline out only when it was needed, but it was always given with love. It seems he was a man of no reserves, no regrets, no retreats, but and most especially and extraordinary, he held in reverence *the ordinary, sacred moments of life.*

It's Only in the Moments

Living a life that matters doesn't happen by accident.
It's not a matter of circumstance but of choice,
because like the speed of light, like the blink of an eye—
with an accuracy known only to God—
life comes and life goes, or so it seems,
and it's then we find ourselves left
with silhouettes of the ordinary sacred.
It's only in the moments, those seemingly insignificant,
that we trace the stages and stations
and recognize that it's now our choice
to keep alive the heartbeat of a life lived well
and honor a death done with dignity.
It's now our choice to follow by example…or not.

Sadly, many of us have observed with clarity
that the darkest waters hold the deepest truths—
metaphor for a man and the miseries endured.
After death, as a family swims through the depths of grief,
we're reminded that we're not called only to proclaim God
but to be the presence of God, reflected,
so that others may come to know and see with new eyes
that the gift of life is more precious through the commonplace.
It's the simple beauty of everyday life, complex and complete,
that we retain, remember, and review.
Rather than rushing on without reverence, without regret,

it's the moments in time when we must fully breathe in
and then give thanks for all that now holds
because soon enough, another day will come,
will crease the dawn with its victory or defeat.

It's only by stopping to celebrate the mystery of life
through an ordinary life that was extraordinary
because of simple truths and small graces
that we can more truly sense the presence of the great I AM.
He takes us just as we are, from wherever we come
and waits on us, to comfort, to hold, to heal,
as He fills us with love, hope, mercy, and renewed joy
so that when we face the next sunrise,
we are able to do so in sacrosanct silence
savoring His presence in each given moment.

I Just Know It: The Faith of a Child

"And He called a child to Himself and set him before them, and said, 'Truly I say to you, unless you are converted and become like children, you will not enter the kingdom of heaven. Whoever then humbles himself as this child, he is the greatest in the kingdom of heaven.'"

—Matthew 18:2–4

She had lived at home as a small child but the family reported that because of the times, financial concerns, her mental capabilities, and who knows what else, she had been placed and lived in a facility her whole life. When we met her, she was well into the latter years of life but had remained child-like, innocent, and content through them all. She obviously had been placed well, received excellent care over her lifetime, because she grew to be a kind, loving, sweet woman with a faith second to none.

I first met her at the facility where she was sitting at a table, working on a puzzle. I introduced myself and she smiled, tipping her head in a study of me, curious about why I was there I supposed. The staff indicated that she could communicate at approximately a six-year-old level, and so, I told her who I was and that I was there to get to know her better. She turned her attention to and began working on the puzzle in front of her. I wondered how many people had come and gone from her life over the years, leaving her with "missing pieces" in what perhaps seemed a puzzle to her.

I asked if working on puzzles was fun, and she replied, "Yes." I asked if she'd like me to help her and she handed me a piece. And so I sat quietly with her for a while, picking up pieces moving them around as if to place them. When she took one out of my hands and placed it in one of the spots I'd passed over, I realized she was more alert than I'd given her credit. I'd been wondering how to approach her, how to broach the questions I needed to ask for her spiritual assessment. Her cockeyed smile out of the corner of her mouth let me know that she knew this puzzle and I wasn't going to put anything over on her. I laughed out loud and she handed me another piece. And so began our relationship—a humbled chaplain and an eighty-plus-year-old child.

She put me in my place on more than one occasion, and always because of her faith.

Like the time I asked her if she knew about heaven and where it was; she snorted and pointed up to the ceiling.

I asked, *"What do you know about heaven?"*

"It's where Jesus lives," she replied matter-of-factly.

"How do you know that?" I queried further.

With a shrug of her shoulders, she said, *"I don't know, I just know it."*

She helped me become more aware of my own faith and how I'd come to believe what I accept as true. In private, I wondered how she had been able to connect with Jesus and then hold her faith through the years: moving from one facility to another; through the countless number of caretakers she'd known and grown attached to and then "lost" as they'd moved on; and now through the trials of aging and disease?

It was obvious she had some religious/spiritual training, or in the least had heard the Word of God, because she could tell bits and pieces of stories from the Bible. Perhaps Proverbs 22:6 explains it the best: *"Train up a child in the way he should go, even when he is old he will not depart from it."* She also taught me as Romans 10:17 declares: *"So faith comes from hearing, and hearing by the word of Christ."* I don't know how I know it. I just know it's true.

It came down to this:

an 8 by 10 cubicle
warm and comfortable
but not home.
A twin bed took one wall,
with a three-drawer dresser.
The recliner faced a window,
where a TV sat on a stand
alongside her Bible.
A favorite painting
and a display of photos
decorated grey walls.
Jesus hung there, too,
reassuring: *"The way*
may be difficult at times,
but I will always be with you."
A roommate snored
behind the curtain,
a sound of life nearby;
fresh flowers graced
the room's loneliness,
spoke love and reminded
that someone from somewhere
remembered she was still alive.

Taking for Granted

"Show us your lovingkindness, O LORD, and grant us Your Salvation."

—Psalm 85:7

It's most humbling when someone young goes before us much older and in a bizarre way; we find our hearts and faith are shaken to their depths. That's because in our humanness/the flesh, we plan our lives by looking to tomorrow. Sadly in the process, we miss today, take things for granted, and forget to think about or prepare for the time when as Paul recorded in 1 Thessalonians 5, *"For you yourselves know full well that the day of the Lord will come just like a thief in the night."*

Well, the thief came that December, sooner than anyone would have imagined, leaving a community of people stunned, broken-hearted, confused, angry, unable to wrap their minds and thoughts around all the emotions. All anyone knew for sure was it hurt. Further down in chapter 5 of Thessalonians, Paul reminds us that despite our best intentions and plans laid out, none will escape death, but then he shines a light of hope with the words, *"You, brethren, are not in darkness...you are all sons of light and sons of day...and since we are of the day, let us put on the breastplate of faith and love, and as a helmet, the hope of salvation. For God has not destined us for wrath, but for obtaining salvation through our Lord Jesus Christ, who died for us, so that whether we are awake or asleep, we will live together with Him."*

A song, titled "I Can Only Imagine," speaks to how a man anticipates responding to his ultimate destination, and it makes us wonder if we'll be ready or not. It's the matter that we all put off thinking about because it's too hard, too much to even try to imagine, so we mostly avoid the subject. This young man met his fate/ day of judgment sooner than any of us could have imagined, but it seems he is one of the few who was more fully aware and the reason he chose to live his days to the fullest until that time he was to be called home. It reads: *"Today I have given you the choice between life and death, between blessings and curses. Now I call on heaven and earth to witness the choice you make. Oh, that you would choose life so that you and your descendants might live!"* (Deuteronomy 30:19).

Oh, that you would choose life so that you and your descendants might live is exactly why we gathered that day. Not because a man died, but because he had lived. As I sat with his family that week, there were a couple of truths that kept coming to the top. First I was reminded: God is a four-letter word spelled L-O-V-E. And Scripture tells us that love covers all, separates us from others, edifies us, is kind, casts out fear, and never fails. This young man walked, talked, and shared his love wide open, full speed ahead, whether it was for his family, his work, his hobbies, his friends, or the days he was granted.

And second, while we know we shouldn't take anything for granted, a brother spoke the truth: *"What we're going to miss the most about him are those things that we took for granted all these years."* And it's those "things about him" that set him apart that spoke to a connection that he seemed to have with God that didn't come from attending a church but was purposed in his heart from the beginning. It seems he was a son of light and a son of day…and he wore a breastplate of faith and love and a helmet of hope for salvation, for God had not destined him for wrath but for joy and life, to which he gave his all.

From the beginning, he was a little man, the independent one. He wouldn't even let his mother walk him to his kindergarten classroom the first day of school. *He could do this on his own.* To which siblings added, he always paved the way, whether in school or sports or whatever. He was a protector, and they told about a neighborhood outdoor slumber party—the guys in a tent in one back yard with the girls in their tent in the other yard. When one of the girls screamed, without a thought, he literally leaped over a pretty high fence to see what was wrong. A brother laughed in the retelling, remembering he then had to walk all the way around the house to get back to his tent because the fence was too tall to even crawl over.

He was a sports kind of guy and loved music. After he went to work in the oil field and because he was such a people person, his family believed he loved his work because of the like-minded guys he got to work with. As with everything in his life, they said he took great pride in what he did and gave it his all and made many good friends along the way.

His wife said he entered their marriage, their love story with an attitude that made others believe in marriage. He was a man who loved to take chances because each day was a new adventure to him; they'd often get stuck someplace and have to call for help to be dug out. But then they became parents. She said his emotional side came out. His attitude changed in that his whole world became his children and not taking anything for granted. He began to live with less abandon, pay attention to the moments. He often spoke, "Why dwell on the negatives; everybody has troubles in their lives; everybody faces tough times," so he chose to meet trials head on and focus on: *"Whatever things are true...honorable...right...pure...lovely and of good report, if there is any virtue and if there is anything praiseworthy; meditate on these things"* (Philippians 4:8).

His family said he was honest, a man of integrity. If he liked you, you knew it, and if he didn't, you knew it. There was nothing phony about him. The family agreed he wasn't a saint, nor did he get it right all the time because he was human in every way. However and despite the fact that he was not a regular church-goer, he nevertheless proved to be a deeply spiritual and Godly man. His life was his testimony. Just as is recorded in Luke 8:15, *"But the seed in the good soil, these are the ones who have heard the Word with an honest and good heart, and hold it fast, and bear fruit with perseverance."*

He remained true and obedient to the ideals he'd grown up with, those he hoped his children would learn. In the very least, his death certainly made others take a second look at who and what God is and how He's relevant and important to our lives. Before us was the testimony of this one man's walk…one loving, cheerful, giving man, kind and faithful, solid as a rock; one who accepted the days he was given and enjoyed them to the fullest, not taking anything for granted.

Precious and sacred
are the times of our lives
those moments of love
that we float through unaware
leave unnoticed
take for granted.

Precious and sacred
are the moments we miss
in the rush and the roar
tossing them aside
empty and unnoticed
taken for granted.

Bearing Fruit with Perseverance

"And we have known and believed the love that God has for us.
God is love, and he who abides in love abides in God and God in him."

—1 John 4:16

I need to clarify that while I don't know much about anything, I do know the love of God when I see it in action, and believe me, He and His love are alive and well. I observed Him in action several ways that week: first in the shocked looks on faces and when the tears welled up from the hearts of friends and neighbors when they heard the news. God went to work through the too-many-to-name loving hands that prepared meals, dropped by to see if there was anything that needed done, or simply just did something that needed done. I most especially saw His love manifest itself through the love of sons, brothers who stood holding hands with one another in a circle around their mother as they bowed their heads in prayer, letting their tears fall freely and openly. And then I observed God's strength and courage in action as they raised their heads and expressed gratefulness that the man, their husband and father whom they loved so dearly, was able to go doing what he loved, on the place that he loved, rather than having to die an old or helpless man, dependent on others for his care.

Stunned is the mildest word I could find for expressing what this family experienced. A sudden death, his was most definitely one of those times that stops all of us in our tracks and makes us take a good, long, hard look at life. For cynics and nonbelievers, his was a day to be sad and mournful, maybe curse the gods they claimed not to believe in. The theory is, *you live your life, then you die, and damn the luck.*

However, for those who believe in or hold hope for the possibility of Jesus and life after death, his was a day to grieve, yes, but it was also a day to celebrate because it meant he was off on a new and the greatest adventure of his lifetime. I told them, "There isn't anything I or any of us can say or do today that will change his outcome; he made his choices and he's in God's hands now. However, it's my intention and prayer to try to help you, the living, find some comfort and hope as you remember the life of a husband, father, grandfather, neighbor and friend and how he chose to live out his time."

None of us tried to make him out to be a saint or even more than he was, because he was human in every way; however, he had proven himself to be not only a good man but a Godly man, and we knew that to be true by the choices he made and the example he set.

His family asked me to help others remember that what he taught was love of family and moral values. He didn't preach; he simply walked out the virtues he believed to be right and true, hoping that others heard what was being said. I was reminded of Luke 8:11–15 and the parable of the seed as the word of God: *"Those seeds beside the road are those who have heard, but the devil comes and takes away the word from their heart; those on the rocky soil hear, and receive the word with joy, but there's no firm root, so they believe for a while then temptation pulls them away. There's seed that falls among the thorns, which are choked with worries and the pleasures of this life, so no fruit comes to maturity. But the seed in the good soil, these are the ones who have heard the word in an honest and good heart, and hold it fast, and bear fruit with perseverance."*

Family said he wasn't afraid of anything—evidenced through his buying his first piece of ground at age seventeen. He ranched and farmed his entire life, was a true stockman who had a passion for taking care of his cattle and his land. He had been raised with the ethic and the fact that he and his family (and many of his neighbors who were present at his funeral) were in the livestock business to feed the nation. It was less about how much money he'd make, and more about the quality of the cow he produced. He took great pride in his life's work, loved what he did and through every season.

In addition, the example that family and friends said they most respected about him was his integrity. They said he was so honest that if he came home from town with an extra something or other in the sack, he would get back in the car and go back to the store to pay for it. Even if it was only a $20 item, he wouldn't jip anyone out of anything for any amount of money.

It was his best friend who first spoke about his ability to overcome and persevere. He mentioned a 10 year coin from Alcoholics Anonymous. That opened the door for others to come forward and speak to this man's dedication to the AA meetings and the number of people he had helped and encouraged through their addictions over the years. Many gave him credit for their own success in overcoming. They all agreed that he was a man whom Paul described in Romans 5:3–5, *"Knowing that tribulation brings about perseverance, and perseverance, proven character, and proven character hope, and hope does not disappoint, because the love of God has been poured out within our hearts through the Holy Spirit who was given to us."*

This man made his choices in life, and by the size of the crowd present at his funeral, it was obvious more of those decisions had been good, and by that I mean: forgiving, right, kind, gentle, loving, and hospitable. What a legacy he left that others might see and hear God's word being lived out through the life of one ordinary, common man who *heard the word in an honest and good heart, held it fast, and bore fruit with perseverance.*

Waiting on God

"They who wait for the Lord
shall renew their strength."

—Isaiah 40:31

To wait upon God is entirely within the reach of all, whatever the age, condition or environment; anyone, Christian or otherwise, can wait upon the Lord. However, it's not ever as easy to carry through as it is to read or hear that truth preached. While the Bible tells us much about waiting upon the Lord, one long-term and ninety-eight-year-old, favorite resident at the hospice house brought this teaching home for us. She was a good and faithful Christian woman who either forgot the parts of Scripture that referenced waiting, or because she'd been waiting for what seemed like years, she sometimes became impatient.

We came to understand this about her and delighted in her reactions and behavior as her health issues allowed her to be with us for longer than the usual six month requirement and eligibility for hospice. We learned early on that she was a woman of great faith but it was her ability to find humor in waiting on God that was what I came to love most about her personality.

The first meaning of the expression "waiting on God" is silence. Once a prayer has been made, the soul is to hush, bow in silence (in faith), and wait before God. She was always okay with the prayer part

94

but not so much with the silence piece. She delighted me and others with her quick-witted observations which would go something like:

> *"So what are you up to today?"*
> *"Oh not much, just taking in the day here in the train station, waiting on God."*

She was no different than any other human in that age doesn't mean much once we've made up our minds and accepted something. She accepted that she was dying, expressed no fear about it at all; her faith remained strong. However, her soul was restless and noisy. After months of waiting, her heart became distressed and burdened; she decided she wasn't worthy of being with God or going to heaven. So I changed her plan of care, began going to prayer more often with her and did what I could to encourage her through God's Word: *"For God alone my soul waits in silence, for my hope is from him"* (Psalm 62:1, 5).

Then she began telling staff, *"I'm just gonna sit here and wait in silence for that chariot to swing low."*

To wait upon God means to expect from God; it implies dependence. But again, the natural woman is so self-sufficient. She began to expect help from her natural ability, from friends, or from the staff. In the spiritual realm, she had been taught to distrust self and to depend upon the power of the Holy Spirit, so she'd put it to the test by saying, *"Think I'll just go trust God in my recliner. His Holy Spirit will find me there."*

She was well read and studied in the Bible and would often-times speak Psalms and memorized verses from heart. One such verse was Proverbs 8:34: *"Blessed is the man who listens to me, watching daily at my gates, waiting beside my doors."* So for a while she'd ask if she could go sit out front and wait by the *"gate"* for that *"sweet by and by."*

Scripture also tells us that man is not to understand the movement of God in the world. But it's hard for us in our fallen conditions to remember that truth. Yes, we may recognize the wonderful blessings in our lives and so are better able to wait; however, once this dear woman made up her mind she was dying and she was okay with that, she thought it should happen "now." Bless her heart, she spent many an hour waiting on God to come and take her home. The good news was, when He finally did, she was able to go peacefully and quietly. However, I've often wondered what her first words were when she got to the other side.

Dying Breaths

Her last and parting question—
woman, wife, one mother to another,
hospice patient to chaplain—
How do I manage the breaths?
Do I save them for the good days
for trips to Dubois and the mountains,
or do I begin to use them every day?

Do I let them carry me forward
or do I begin to count them,
draw them in deliberately,
try not to waste a solitary one?
And left unspoken but clearly heard—
how do I manage the breaths
before the last, dying one?

The only answer I have to offer
just as the Lord God formed you,
breathed into you the breath of life (Gen. 2:7)
ordained your life is but a breath (Job 7:7)
Jesus breathes for you and that believing
you will have life in His name (John 20:22)
so breathe deeply, my friend, breathe deeply!

If I Die Young

If I die young, bury me in satin, lay me down on a bed of roses.
Sink me in the river at dawn, send me away
with the words of a love song.
The sharp knife of a short life, well, I've had just enough time
So put on your best, boys, and I'll wear my pearls.
And I'll be wearing white when I come into your kingdom.

It was a winter's Monday afternoon, and I had just finished paying tribute to a member of our community at a funeral. A husband and son were in the audience without their wife and mother who insisted that they go to the service in support of their friend instead of going to the doctor's appointment with her; she insisted that the highways would be okay. Then came the phone call—that unspeakable call from most human's world of worst fears.

My call came later from the funeral home. I started talking to God, praying and questioning: "What? She's so young. Why, Lord? What's this all about? Why are you bringing me to this, this to me?" And then I was welcomed into a home, into a family circle.

As this family's tears flowed and their thoughts came tumbling out, there wasn't one "why" or "what's this all about" or word of anger spoken. Only the words of *life, light, laughter,* and *loving kindness* were spoken, were clearly how this woman had lived, how her family functioned. I knew within a short while why God had brought me to them, to this. I understood, at least in part, that it's those words that needed to be shared so that God's light, loving kindness, and promises of life could be illuminated—more clearly seen and understood.

You see our God doesn't cause accidents, but He certainly uses them to speak to us, to remind us He is with us in all things, to remind us that He knows our hearts, knows our sorrows, shares our pain, and that He's right here to see us through if we but call on Him.

The family chose her favorite song, "If I Die Young" by Band Perry, from which I pulled lyrics. I also chose to use the "string of pearls" referred to as The Beatitudes found in Matthew 5, followed by a reference to "salt and light," both of which I believed were pertinent for how this woman chose to live with love leading the way.

In Matthew 5, Jesus is speaking to his disciples and the multitudes who are wondering, questioning, "Who is this man and what can He possibly say that pertains to me and my life?"

Blessed are the poor in spirit for theirs is the kingdom of heaven.
Blessed are they who mourn for they shall be comforted.
Blessed are the meek for they shall inherit the earth.
Blessed are they who hunger and thirst for righteousness for they shall be satisfied.
Blessed are the merciful for they shall receive mercy.
Blessed are the pure in heart for they shall see God.
Blessed are the peacemakers for they shall be called the children of God.
Blessed are those who have been persecuted for righteousness' sake for theirs is the kingdom of Heaven.
Blessed are you when men persecute you and say all manner of evil against you falsely for my sake.
Rejoice and be glad for great is your reward in heaven…

I revealed that the word "blessed" in its original intention means "fully satisfied" and indicates a purity of heart, a peacemaker attitude. What the family and friends began to share at her service was that she was blessing, a believer who had experienced the peace of God and who brought that peace to her fellow human beings. They said she lived in a state of blessedness which began the moment she believed in Jesus Christ. And it's Him who calls those who believe, *"The salt of the earth…and the light of the world,"* and tells us, *"nor does anyone light a candle and put it under a basket, but on a candlestick so that it gives light to all that are in the house."* Further He says, *"Let your light shine before men that they may see your good works and glorify Your Father who is in heaven."*

That's how this young woman chose to live, sharing the blessings—the salt and the light to anyone and everyone with whom she came into contact. The kids in her blended family, all five of them plus some in-laws, said that she was like a light that came into their lives and changed everything, making it a better place for them. They said, "She accepted us all, just as we are, and she was always there for us, no matter what." They said she made sure everybody was taken care of and safe. As her car careened across a patch of ice that Monday, her final attempt to keep one of them safe was an arm stretched full across a chest to hold and protect with the words, "Hang on!"

Who would have thought forever could be severed by
the sharp knife of a short life, well, I've had just enough time.

I told the crowd gathered at her funeral, "As members of God's family, as members of this community, we—you and I, every one of us in this room—have felt the shock; we can choose to curl up and shut off the world, or we can choose to hang on and live from her example, learn from this family's courage. We can focus on helping one another by reaching out with loving kindness, letting our light shine with laughter, and by living life to the fullest. We can choose to begin anew each day and how we plan to handle what comes our way, because we won't know when we've had enough time. And when we don't know what to say or what to do to help this family or any family, we can always pray. Pray like we've never prayed before.

"That's how we can in part make sense of this that seems so senseless."

There was a next part—a good that had already come from a young woman's death. The family was most especially humbled by and asked me to share that she was an organ donor.

Because of her belief that her body was merely a temporary home and her courage in that regard, the circumstances were such that her eyes were already helping somebody else see; two children's lives were saved from her heart alone; the potential was that over one hundred people might benefit, perhaps have their health and conceivably their very life restored in part because of her love for doing for others.

She chose to purpose her life by being willing to give that others might live. And so rather than thinking of her light as going out on that Monday, I suggested that her light will actually be shining always and forever brighter. I felt it would continue to shine through the lifetime of all who loved her so well through the beautiful memories she left as her legacy!

So put on your best, boys, and I'll wear my pearls
what I never did is done, and maybe then you'll hear the words
I been singing, the ballad of a dove...go with peace and love.

Song lyrics excerpted from "If I Die Young" by Kimberly Perry, Published by Lyrics © Sony/ATV Music Publishing LLC

Living with False Guilt

"And I said, 'O my God, I am ashamed and embarrassed to lift up my face to You, my God, for my iniquities have risen above my head and my guilt has grown even to the heavens.'"

—Ezra 9:6

She had been in our care for a few months, and I had grown especially fond of her because she had a quick wit, always acted pleased when I came to visit, was interested in hearing what was happening in the community and with me personally, and she was ever so grateful for all the attention and care that we had brought to her otherwise isolated and what I deemed a lonely life. She and I had friends and interests in common, and so striking up a conversation was never an issue. Having said all that, it wasn't long before a spiritual concern for this woman arose, and in my opinion, proved to be a primary factor for her overall well-being.

My initial spiritual plan of care for her regarding faith was "affirmation of patient's present level of spiritual comfort." Simply defined that meant she was a woman of faith, had articulated her belief in God, and said she had no fear of dying. So my first goal was to support and encourage her in said faith.

However, over time, hints of uncertainty in that regard began to creep into our discussions. Always, though, no matter how I approached the matter of God's love for her or her worthiness, she'd brush me off, hold in any emotion she was feeling, and change the subject.

Finally one day, after I paid her a compliment, she told me straight out that she wasn't worthy of God's love or going to heaven and that I made her out to be a better person than she was. She threw those statements out matter-of-factly, with little emotion. There it was, the red flag. I scooted my chair over closer to hers, took her hand, and asked why, but once again she brushed me off, changed the subject, and started talking about something else. But tears had welled up in her eyes.

I changed my plan of care and shared the conversation and concerns with the staff so that we would all be more aware of this facet of her well-being and our caregiving strategies. Not wanting to push her too hard and perhaps away, I simply continued to visit; with each subsequent visit, I would share some Scripture or inspirational reading, reassure her of God's love and grace/forgiveness, and encourage, talk and pray with her, and waited. I realized that trust takes time to build. And thank the Lord, He provided the time.

Once she opened up and shared her story, the whole of it, I came to better understand this woman. For too many years to count she had lived feeling *"rejected, for she found no place for repentance, though she sought for it with tears"* (Hebrews 12:17). It broke my heart when she explained that she had lived with a very low self-image, feelings of inadequacy, and a certainty that she wasn't worthy of love her whole adult life. She admitted that she was too "stubborn and hard-headed" to give in to the weakness of feeling sorry for herself. She told about leaving home at the age of fifteen and going to work. By the time she was eighteen, she had married an abusive man, a drinker who "kept me pregnant to keep control over me."

She said, "I didn't need to be kept by an abusive man, but I knew there was no way I could feed my children; there was no Medicaid in those days to help me care for them. I was too busy to think about faith; I was just trying to stay alive." So she worked harder "as a waitress, an office worker, a bartender, truck driver, whatever I could find to keep a roof over our heads."

She discarded the word "courage," repeating that she was just too stubborn and hard-headed to give up. She told me she later remarried and had been happy with him, but when she lost a son to cancer, she just reasoned that that was God's way of punishing her for all the things she'd done wrong. For her and the balance of her life, there was no freedom from guilt.

Speaking about this complex and all-to-common issue for mankind, well-known evangelist, Billy Graham speaks to guilt with these words: *"Humans are helpless to detach themselves from the gnawing guilt of a heart bowed down with the weight of sin. But where humans have failed, God has succeeded."*

My prayer for her from then on came from Psalm 51 and was the way I began an attempt to reassure her of God's love and forgiveness. *"Create in me a clean heart, O God, and renew a steadfast spirit within me. Do not cast me away from Your presence and do not take Your Holy Spirit from me. Restore to me the joy of Your salvation and sustain me with a willing spirit"* (v. 10–12).

The sad truth is, my attempts didn't help at all; her final days were fraught with restlessness and pain. She simply could not or would not allow herself to get past her guilt, nor could she or would she trust God's forgiveness: *"And I said, 'O my God, I am ashamed and embarrassed to lift up my face to You, my God, for my iniquities have risen above my head and my guilt has grown even to the heavens.'"*

The Burden

(Nehemiah 9:17)

She told me once that the only thing
she ever stole was a Bible from the store.
Too young to grasp all the implications
she understood all too well why
her father made her take it back, apologize.
Who could have foreseen that lone incident
would be a foreshadowing of the ill will
she'd forever hold for her Heavenly Father—
that which was built on guilt.

The burden became a word she wouldn't trust,
never felt was meant for her, so she found fault
in herself—felt unworthy all her life—
wore it like a shawl, frayed and worn through.
She never did perceive the presence of
"Forgiveness: gracious, compassionate, slow
to anger, abounding in lovingkindness."
She refused to listen or hope that God would
"neither leave nor forsake her."

Letting Go and Letting God

"For God has not given us a spirit of fear, but of power and of love and of a sound mind."

—2 Timothy 1:7

Fear is one of the enemy's most popular weapons that he uses against us. Worry, anxiety, and fear can overwhelm us with a thick shadow of darkness, controlling our every decision and move. Whether we recognize and acknowledge it or not, our walk through life is a singular effort. Oh yes, it's wonderful when we have companions to help us, to encourage and hold us accountable, to share the times along our walks, but we must be aware that it's human nature to become too attached to things or people—even if we know that they are not good for us, even and especially when we realize that at some point we have to give up but haven't yet learned how to let go.

Reality tells us that so much of what we spend our time worrying about never even happens. Living under the weight of the "what if's" is a hard place to dwell. So is choosing to allow fear and anxiety to control our life. It is unfortunate to realize that many people who suffer in the same way he did will never learn how to curb their own suffering. John tells us clearly in 1 John 4:18, *"There is no fear in love. But perfect love drives out fear because fear has to do with punishment."*

Why is it so difficult to let go? It's not easy to let go or overcome fear, but it always comes down to a choice. The truth is most of us suffer from a feeling of inner emptiness that we are trying to

106

fill up with our various attachments—often without much success. One person may eat too much, another may cling to a partner, while a third may become addicted. But none of these can fill our inner emptiness. It's amazing how much we can deceive ourselves, believing that things and people will bring us happiness when, in reality, it was never the case. His was no different and fear and anxiety were the indicators.

Day 1: He expressed that he was very worried about leaving his wife and daughter. He told the staff the two women were his whole world. Their love was a blessing for him and his expression of it was endearing. Except, he was so anxious about leaving them that he needed medication to calm down.

Day 2: He remained alert, able to and privately asked his daughter to take care of his wife, and later, also in private, asked his wife to watch over his daughter. Both very normal and loving behaviors; however, he told the nurse what he'd done, as well as a CNA, the chaplain, and the social worker. He was overly worried about how they would get along without him taking care of them, even after they had both tried to reassure him that they would be okay. It was as if he needed approval or applause. What he certainly needed was extra attention.

Day 3: He began to express worry about his wife's health, her well-being; began talking to staff about her health issues, wanted to get her help, all the while deflecting questions about dying and his emotional and spiritual well-being. He wouldn't accept offers or allow himself to be calmed. His anxiety was obvious as restlessness, nervous chatter, not wanting to go to sleep, making sure there was someone in the room with him at all times. He told the nurse he wasn't in any pain, but his inability to be calmed even with medication, even with them by his side, indicated his was pain of a different kind. He constantly pushed the call button, kept the staff running and the two women he clung to in turmoil that day. They became anxious because of his suffering. They reassured him that they would be okay. They told him it was okay for him to go. We prayed over him, brought music into his room, tried shutting the door for privacy, tried opening the door so he could see out. Nothing seemed to help him relax.

Day 4: Death didn't come peacefully for this man, despite the fact that his family remained at his bedside the whole time. He continued to verbalize his love for them, but finally came the delayed truth—his fear of leaving them and life as he'd known it. He was scared to die, and there was no consoling him. There was nothing any of us could do to help him. He waited until the last few hours of life to talk about his concerns openly, but he wouldn't let go, despite Jesus's reconciliatory promise as recorded in Philippians 4:6–7, *"Do not be anxious about anything, but in every situation, by prayer and petition, with thanksgiving, present your requests to God. And the peace of God, which transcends all understanding, will guard your hearts and your minds in Christ Jesus."* He couldn't or wouldn't make a decision to let go of his fear by letting God in.

As an ambassador for Christ, I sat by feeling helpless because this man wouldn't hear what God's Word has to say: "For by grace you have been saved through faith; and that not of yourselves, it is the gift of God" (Ephesians 2:8). He simply wouldn't trust, *"Lord, for what do I wait? My hope is in You"* (Psalm 39:7). He wouldn't consider: *"So do not fear, for I am with you; do not be dismayed, for I am your God"* (Isaiah 41:10).

As for the rest of us, those still living in the day to day, there might be times we feel afraid, but we can believe that God is with us. We may not be in control, but we can trust the One who is. We may not know the future, but we can know the God who does. And while there's nothing magical about words and verses, there is power through them because they're God's words. Change happens. Anxious thoughts begin to diminish. Worry, let go of its constant grip. And though fear is sometimes still there, it no longer wields control, holding one back, paralyzing in its grasp. Jesus's words are "life" words, soothing to one's soul, calming to one's spirit, giving power to one's days if we but choose to hear them. First Peter 5:6–7 suggests: *"Humble yourselves, therefore, under God's mighty hand, that he may lift you up in due time. Cast all your anxiety on him because he cares for you."*

It's Enough

*"And He has said to me, 'My Grace is sufficient for
you, for power is perfected in weakness.'"*

—2 Corinthians 12:9–10

When he first came into hospice care, he reassured me as Chaplain
that he had plenty of spiritual encouragement because one of his
family members was his minister. He expressed contentment in his
faith and helped me choose the initial, spiritual plan of care. He liked
the idea and plan that speaks to the Chaplain being available PRN
(on call) to affirm the present level of spiritual comfort and support.
His decision was an indication that even though he was dying, he
was still able to advocate for himself and wanted to have some say
regarding the care he would receive during his final days.

It was several days later when I called to set the next appointment with him; however, by then, we were in a late, below zero and
brittle December period. All the same, this man warmed my heart in
ways that can only be explained through Grace. Still able to speak for
himself and proving to be a true gentleman, he said he didn't want
me coming out in the cold but asked if we could have our visit over
the phone.

Christmas was a week away so I asked if his family had set any
special plans, if he was looking forward to the celebration. His honesty was enlightening: "This year for some reason, I'm more in tune
with what Christmas is all about than ever before. It's certainly not

about dinners, trees, carols, or presents. Do you think it's because I'm ninety that I'm finally figuring it out?" He went on to say that being at home where it's warm and comfortable in every way was "enough." He was content in his place—physical, emotional, and spiritual, his lot in life—and was simply living out the days as they came and went. He held no expectations beyond that.

It's humbling to spend time with the dying who are so faith-filled that even in the waves of the dying process are able to communicate: *"Enough, My Grace is sufficient for you."* It was through Grace that this man was able to express his faith and his love for mankind and be thoughtful about others and their well-being above his own. He was an inspiration, a courageous soul anticipating and hopeful for heaven when it was time, *"for Christ's sake (he) delighted in his weakness…for in that weakness, he was strong."*

Life Is Just a Little While

"And to know the love of Christ which surpasses knowledge, that at last you may be filled up to all the fullness of God."

—Ephesians 3:19

He spent his remaining time on earth with us through one summer. Self-described as "the ugliest man from Montana," I found just the opposite to be true. From the first time I met him, I liked him. He was a tease and a flirt, a man with a quick wit and a love for God, his family, and life that superseded everything else. Because he'd been a truck driver for much of his life, he related to radio personality and songwriter, Red Sovine, who wrote a prayer that he said he'd like read at his funeral:

> *Dear God above, bless this truck I drive and help me keep someone alive. Be my mortal sight this day on the street where little children play. Bless my helper fast asleep when the night is long and keep my cargo safe and sound through the hours big and round. Make my judgment sound as steel and be my hands upon the wheel. Bless the traveler going past and teach them not to go so fast. Give me strength for every trip so I may care for what they ship. And make me mindful every mile that life is just a little while. Amen.*

In his early years, he told me he did odd jobs including working at the Parks Department, as a timber jack, a milk delivery man, in a cheese factory, and construction work. He became owner and operator of his own trucking company but told his family that his biggest job and hobby was saving money. He proudly told that he could make a dollar stretch further than most people and delighted in finding ways to do so. He made sure his bills were paid in advance and enjoyed "barrow pit" shopping, saying, "You never know when you might need that," regarding whatever great find he'd come home with. He'd been married "a time or two" but admitted it was hard for women to stay married to a man who was always gone. His last companion was a faithful and loving dachshund who was always by his side.

He chose to live out his life as the quoted excerpts from a poem by Graeme Cook:

"There's a callous on his thumb from the splitter 'neath the gear-knob that seems molded to his hand. Pain stayed in his back from the years upon the track; his tired old driver's seat became shaped to fit that back, for making up the miles was all that mattered. His roads were never easy, dusty, bumpy, wet and greasy, and no load ever simple, just simply bloody hard; he'd more than once been there and back, seen every destination, and would to all the toughest jobs respond. He carried memories of loads and places that he'd been, his life was filled with people, all grateful for him living. He loved a quiet beer or two, and his children close at hand; these are the things in life that brought him smiles. He chose to find pleasure in simple things; chose to be filled up with God himself."[7]

Toward the end of that summer, he decided to make one last road trip. A daughter drove him south; let him have one last look around the region he'd traveled so often. When he got tired, he asked her to bring him home. She said he crawled into his recliner with his faithful companion in his lap, and she found them that way the next morning. The measure of the man was perhaps most clearly and

---

[7.] Excepted from "Andy's Miles" by Graeme Cook.

sincerely explained when we had to peel the dog off his lap so the funeral director could take him away.

It was that incident and a simple prayer that helped remind me and the other staff who worked with him that we need to be ever mindful that life is just a little while, and we have the choice to live it out filled up with God himself or not.

Living a Life That Matters

"No one has seen God at any time; if we love one another,
God abides in us, and His love is perfected in us.
And He has put his own Holy Spirit into our hearts as a
proof to us that we are living with him and He with us."

—1 John 4:12–13

It's always humbling to preside at a funeral (or attempt to write someone's story) because it's difficult to speak about an individual and how they chose to live out their life. There are those times, however, when it's easier because some people simply live bigger, choose to live a life that matters. It's those individuals who leave behind a rich and wonderful inheritance that inspires others of us to do the same.

One of the problems I face trying to encapsulate a story is to find a way to put all of the individual into a "box." In this case, it appeared he was a combination of Pecos Bill, Superman, Paul Bunyan, and Forrest Gump. His story was rather like Gump's box of chocolates; he didn't fit into any one square.

So how to start? In the beginning God created the heavens and the earth, brought forth vegetation and living waters, brought forth living creatures, then created man in His own image, and God saw that it was good. However, not all of life was or is good to all of His people. In this case this man left home at age thirteen after an incident with yet another step-father. He didn't keep his biological father's name, but rather chose to carry the one from the nicest step-father. He found work, spent some time in the Navy, and then headed to Wyoming looking for a brother. It's where he fell in love, married, and began to raise a family and make his living.

His family said he could have used his youth as an excuse to become a sullen man or an outlaw or turn just plain mean. But no, that wasn't the case. He had the ability to find something humorous in every situation, make others laugh, and he never complained. He made the conscious choice to love and live his life as a man who fought for what was right and as a result became a guardian angel to many people.

There's a poem "Live a Life That Matters" by Michael Josephson that talks about the measure of a man and the last two lines are: *Living a life that matters doesn't happen by accident. It's not a matter of circumstance but of choice.* What I learned from this man was that he chose to live a life that mattered, regardless of his circumstances. As a rescuer, he made himself available anywhere, everywhere, any time, every time. Whether it was a complicated rescue of someone from a fire, on a ski slope, or in a car wreck, or a more simple rescue like bringing a set of keys to a daughter who locked herself out of her car, or driving to Billings to pick up an injured grandson, or helping a friend work through some personal issue, he loved people, loved to help people. He never met a stranger, and he never turned down an opportunity to help someone if it was possible for him to do so.

He was a defender of people and doing what was right; because of that, his family said he often got into fights; however, to the best of their knowledge, he didn't usually start them. He just didn't back down from them. He was always defending someone or some important issue. They said he couldn't and wouldn't tolerate the strong picking on the weak. He didn't hold grudges, so once something was settled, it was settled.

He was a hard worker and proved to be a man among men. He was a good friend and honest to a fault. He didn't mince words, didn't say anything derogatory, but told you what was on his mind and was honest in what he was saying. You always knew where you stood with him. At the same time, he had the special gift of being able to put people at ease with a trademark grin and attitude.

Despite the fact that he referred to God as "the practical joker in the sky" and himself as a "friendly agnostic," he ended up telling his family that he had come to believe in and had accepted Jesus Christ. Proving once again that this man who loved to learn, could not and did not stay contained in one box and had finally come to grips with his Creator.

That may have been the final and best explanation, may be the reason why despite a hard childhood, he overcame, went further, and became more to so many against the odds. He kept on trusting God and loving life—even when his heart was broken to the point that he couldn't talk. I'm speaking about when he and his wife lost a son in a tragic accident. Once again, he made a critical choice…he chose life; after all, he was a man of character, a man of courage, a man of God. The Bible tells us: *"No one has seen God at any time; but if we love one another, God abides in us, and His love is perfected in us."* His family believed this man received his reward of eternal life in heaven through his belief in Jesus Christ, his love for others, and a life lived well.

Living a life that matters doesn't happen by accident.
It's not a matter of circumstance but of choice.

It's How She Lived

*"For in it the righteousness of God is revealed from faith to faith;
as it is written, 'But the righteous man shall live by faith.'"*

—Romans 1:17

At what many considered too young an age, she was diagnosed with Alzheimer's.

Because she was so young and healthy otherwise, hers was a long, grueling battle. As her world slowly but surely began to close in around her, her family and community became consumed with one particular question they asked over and over again: "Why? Why? Why?"

I didn't pretend to have an answer then, nor do I now with this writing. What I do know from the Scriptures is that nothing occurs without God's permission (Ephesians 1:11). We also must trust that God is good, so we might conclude that he allows what we perceive as bad things to occur because according to his sovereign plan everything will ultimately work out for His good purposes—especially for those who love Him (Romans 8:28).

What I have come to understand is that we are brought through situations like this so that we can search out and talk about and in the very least help one another with our questions. I've not spent many times with any sadder group of people than after she died. I talked with her husband, sons, father, best friends, a daughter-in-law—same question, same sadness. And yet each of them was able to define, perhaps unaware that they themselves knew/held that which was hidden but was such an obvious answer. It's how she lived: loving, caring, always happy, helpful, attentive, put everybody else's needs first: as a teacher, comforter, cheerleader, supporter, problem solver, with honesty, patience, and kindness. It seemed that for everyone who knew her, they knew what love looked like, behaved like, how it worked and made them feel.

First Corinthians 13:4–7 speaks directly and most clearly to what love is and always will be. The Apostle Paul wrote:

> *Love is patient, love is kind and is not jealous;*
> *love does not brag and is not arrogant,*
> *does not act unbecomingly;*
> *it does not seek its own, is not provoked,*
> *does not take into account a wrong suffered,*
> *does not rejoice in unrighteousness, but rejoices with the truth,*
> *bears all things, believes all things, hopes all things, endures all things.*

Hanging on the refrigerator in this woman's kitchen was a magnet that she kept posted there for as long as anyone could remember; it read: "It's not how much we give but how much love we put into giving." And give with love is what she did. She was a best friend, a help mate, a lover, a cushion when someone needed a safe place to land. Her family talked about how caring she was to them and to everyone. They said she instilled in them a hard work ethic and integrity: "She always expected us to be honest, no matter what." She put them and their needs before hers. A son remembered her as unfailingly happy and their problem solver. He said, "She did everything for us, made our beds, picked up after us, had meals ready whenever we came in, allowed our friends to come and go, and yet, she taught us to be independent too."

They all agreed that she taught them and expected them to be neat and tidy—and that meant not only in their rooms but in the way they dressed, the way they behaved. She taught them to be respectful to everyone, not just older people, but everyone. She would not tolerate rudeness for any reason. She was their Sunday school teacher when they were young and worked to instill a belief in God so that they would have that to carry them through life.

We laughed about her weapon of choice if any of the rules were disobeyed—they don't know how many wooden spoons were broken over the years, but as soon as she found plastic ones, the guys figured that's when they began growing up because it seems plastic hurts worse and won't break. They said she never missed a game or a school meeting or activity they were involved with.

Another Scripture—1 John 4:8 tells us that God is love and that His love is limitless! The more we give, the more we have to give. If we love those whose lives we touch each day, they will know it and pass it on. This then [love] is the way God manifests Himself on earth. It's the main focus of the commandment He sent down with Jesus: *"A new commandment I give to you, that you love one another, even as I have loved you, that you also love one another"* (John 13:34).

Precious memories and tears are what God gave them to help ease their load of grief. Many tears had been shed over the years prior to her death and have been shed since. It's the precious memories that helped her family recall and survive and that's at the heart of God's message as a family remembers the life, the laughter, and the love. It was not about how she died, but how she lived; not what she gained, but what she gave.

The week she died there was an article by Betty Starks Case featured in the local newspaper which included: "God is love; if we look, we might find that love is hiding right out there—all around us—in plain sight." I don't think I was stretching it to say that I believed this woman knew and experienced and displayed love all around her all the time, in plain sight through the behaviors and creativity she exhibited. I believe that's how she, especially through her last few years, bore, believed, hoped, and endured all things. It is indeed how she lived!

Love Is All There Is

*"Beloved, let us love one another, for love is from God,
and whoever loves has been born of God and knows God."*

—1 John 4:7

While the theory is, we hospice caregivers go into homes to help families, oftentimes the reality is, we are the ones who come away blessed after spending time with a family during one of the most critical and precious times in their lives. Because of how I was treated by her in her home, I will forevermore be grateful for the time I spent with one lady consumed by dementia. While I only got to know her in the last months of her life, and despite the fact that she was usually forgetful and confused, what an amazing and delightful woman she was; she truly left a gracious legacy.

She always greeted me with a sweet smile and an "Oh, I know who you are," even though she didn't. It was easy to say she was a woman "filled with pleasure." Unvarying on her off days, I always left her side filled with a quiet happiness because of her sweet spirit and how she and her husband treated me. As defined by her family and friends, she was a woman filled with laughter, chatter, a funny sense of humor, and kindness. She had beautiful blue eyes, an engaging smile, and a big loving heart. It seems those traits were inherently and subtly woven in because they obviously defined what was the heart of this woman, that which we will always remember best about her. She was a strong, courageous, woman, one who felt deeply and loved with everything she had to give. I believe she epitomized the best of the Proverbs 31 woman:

> *"An excellent wife, who can find? For her worth is far above jewels. The heart of her husband trusts in her, and he will have no lack of gain. She does him good and not evil all the days of her life. She looks for wool and flax and works with her hands in delight. She is like merchant ships; she brings her food from afar. She rises also while it is still night and gives food to her household... She girds herself with strength and makes her arms strong... Her lamp does not go out at night... She extends her hand to the poor, and she stretches out her hands to the needy. She is not afraid of the snow for her household... She makes coverings for herself... Strength and dignity are her clothing, and she smiles at the future. She opens her mouth in wisdom, and the teaching of kindness is on her tongue. She looks well to the ways of her household, and does not eat the bread of idleness. Her children rise up and bless her; her husband also, and he praises her... Give her the product of her hands, and let her works praise her in the gates."*

One particular afternoon as I sat and visited with this couple, I began asking them questions. It was a beautiful time well spent as each of them in turn would answer. I believe the most notable response was hers when I asked: "How do you/have you two survived this many years together? What's been the glue that kept you together through the good times and the bad times?"

Before her husband could even open his mouth, she looked right at me and said, "Love." I asked, "What about love? It's a big word?"

She nodded and said, "I know it is, but it's the only thing; it's all there is..." and then losing her thought, she looked over at her husband, looked to him to finish answering for her.

His simple nod caused all three of us to tear up. Nothing else needed to be said.

Scripture tells us a lot about the word "love," including, *"Love the Lord you God; love your neighbor as yourself; abide in My love; the fruit of the Spirit is love; for love is from God; love casts out all fear; God so loved the world; husbands, love your wives; love edifies; love is kind; we love, because He first loved us."* This woman knew and experienced love in her whole being and displayed it all around her all the time, even in her last and the forgetful stage. It was evident that love was certainly and perfectly simple and distinct for her: "It's all there is." There was nothing that could erase the feeling, the hope, that truth from the heart of her soul.

Paul speaks to this in Romans 8:38–39 with these words: *"For I am convinced that neither death, nor life, nor angels, nor principalities, nor things present, nor things to come, nor powers, nor height, nor depth, nor any other created thing, will be able to separate us from the love of God, which is in Christ Jesus our Lord."* Hers was a testimony about how she and her family, especially those last few weeks of her life believed, hoped, and endured all things.

Through It All

"Marriage is to be held in honor through it all..."

—Hebrews 13:4

She smiles as he wobbles into the room
bravely standing upright as he toddles
enroute to this day's new adventure.
Food scatters and milk accidently spills
and he sheepishly apologizes
as he tries to clean up the mess he's made.
She helps him wipe the dribble from his shirt,
pats his face and sweeps her hand through his hair
as he hugs her and thanks her for her help.

They've come full circle—this wife and now toddler
who struggles to stand and hangs on for balance,
determined in his stance and want to move.
Faithful in her love, she follows along,
ever watchful as he goes about his day,
clears his path and picks up after him,
not wanting to intrude or insult but
mindful that he doesn't stumble or fall
during the day-to-day business of living.

She came on board for better and for worse
not really knowing what that meant at all
but loyal in her loving manner and ways
because no matter the age, she was here to stay
to keep and to hold, to love and obey
through the thick and the thin that life has to give.
They've been through it all, together in love,
and she'll be by his side right up to the end
as God's design is not happenstance.

Planting Seeds of Love

*"A time to give birth and a time to die; a time to
plant and a time to uproot what is planted."*

—Ecclesiastes 3:2

The day of his funeral I spoke: *"For nonbelievers, this is a day to be
sad and mournful, maybe curse the gods they claim not to believe in. The
theory is, you live your life and then you die. The end of a good ole soul.
However, over the past couple years I had the privilege of spending some
time with this man in good and deep conversation, so I can speak directly
to the heart of him. He was one who believed in Jesus and His offer of
life after death. So for him, death wasn't something he feared or grieved.
It was simply what it was, a fact of life; he told me once, all living things
die—plants, animals, people. And he shrugged with the telling."* It was
my hope and intention to pay tribute and honor to that hardworking, always smiling, generous, honest farmer and gentle man of faith,
but as always, it was also my intention and prayer that his service
would help the living see the connection between our God in heaven,
one ordinary man's walk here in His kingdom, and how his planting
the seeds of love serves all eternity.

I titled his service "Planting Seeds of Love" because it seemed
this man was great at doing just that. A farmer through and through,
his legacy included more than teaching about a crop of grain or hay
or discerning when to plant and when to uproot what's been planted;
this farmer taught valuable, meaningful lessons about planting and

reaping what we sow through his tender concern for others and by treating others gently and with a sense of humor.

Luke 8:4–15 explains the parable of a sower; it reads: *"The sower went out to sow his seed; and as he sowed, some fell beside the road, and it was trampled underfoot and the birds of the air ate it up. Other seed fell on rocky soil, and as soon as it grew up, it withered away, because it had no moisture. Other seed fell among the thorns; and the thorns grew up with it and choked it out. Other seed fell into the good soil, and grew up, and produced a crop a hundred times as great."*

As Jesus spoke these things, He would call out, *"He who has ears to hear, let him hear."* It was such a perfect contrast for a farmer, especially for a believing farmer and for all believers because the seed Jesus was speaking of is the word of God, and in this case, it was sown in a man's heart at a young age, received as pure joy, took firm root in a good and honest soul, which then held it fast and bore fruit with perseverance.

Perseverance can be defined and measured any number of ways. For this man it meant family and farming. He was blessed (and that was his word) to have married the love of his life and together plant seeds of love and then watch the fruit of their crop grow. And for him, a good crop meant being a good and loving man in all the roles he assumed in his lifetime. He was a grateful man, commented on the concern and watchfulness of the hospice team who helped him, was grateful for every visit, every prayer, every hug.

For this man, a good crop included the love one shares with neighbors and long-time friends. We reap what we sow. According to his friends, that meant playing a lot of cards together, no one bragging about who was the best at any particular game; going hunting together every so often; keeping up your share of the fences, pulling jokes and laughing at yourself and life as often as you could; always being there for one another through the good times and the sad times; sharing and caring enough to bring over a batch of fresh homemade cinnamon rolls hot from the oven, or visiting when a friend's laid up in bed for a few months, or calling to make sure your neighbor's doing okay. In other words, for him friendship was a refreshing crop to plant and could be like a cool drink of water on a hot day.

Did all those words I spoke about him mean it was always easy, always fun, always went perfectly, always meant bumper crops? Not by any stretch of the imagination, but to put it very simply and in perspective, in his own words: *"It has been a good life."* I'm pretty sure no one has the secret to living the good life, but because of his faith, I was reminded that by planting seeds of love—specifically, God's Word deep in our minds and hearts—we certainly do have an advantage, because with it comes a quiet certainty, an expectation of and display of integrity, a special joy and peace that can't be explained any other way, and a hopefulness that extends to eternity.

Ecclesiastes 3 tells us: *God has made everything appropriate in its time. He has also set eternity in our hearts, yet so that man will not find out the work which He has done from the beginning even to the end. I know that there is nothing better for them than to rejoice and to do good in one's lifetime; moreover that every man who eats and drinks sees good in all his labor—it is the gift of God. I know that everything God does will remain forever; there is nothing to add to it and there is nothing to take from it."*

Now Is the Time

Ecclesiastes 3:2/2 Corinthians 6:2b

God tells us in His Word
"There is an appointed time for everything...
a time for every event under heaven."
And his last days proved it true.

He and his wife loved to garden,
planted corn that spring in anticipation
of the sweetness dripping off their chins
when it came ripe in the fall.

However, as life would have it,
cancer interfered, interrupted
their sweet plans which became his last
on the bucket list—fresh corn from the garden.

With each passing day he'd go check
to see if any ears were ready
but it wasn't meant to be, so he endured,
as he waited for his day of salvation.

After he left on that beautiful fall morning,
wife and daughter walked to the garden and
sure enough, the corn was ready.
"Behold, now is the acceptable time" (2 Cor. 6:2b)

Overcoming Hard-Heartedness

*"We have come to share in Christ if we hold firmly
till the end the confidence we had at first."*

—Hebrews 3:14

It was with a humble and pained heart that I stood before a family and community of friends challenged with the sacred commission of attempting to bring hope and comfort to the hearts of a grieving group after a young woman had overdosed on pain medications. The community was deeply saddened and troubled and the parents were experiencing their worst nightmare because a kind-hearted, intelligent, strong-willed, independent, creative, and fun-loving young woman and mother had chosen not to hold fast to or had given up on the belief and truth: *"The eternal God is her dwelling place"* (Deuteronomy 33:27a).

The family had written, "A star is born; a brilliant new star on God's celestial canvas, and it's hard to miss, twinkling brightly with hues of cobalt and azure. Thank you Heavenly Father for this gift." Despite their pain, they said it was not hard to give thanks even though they hurt, even when they didn't understand and despite the issues she'd faced in her life, she had maintained a positive and grateful attitude in her attempts to overcome those issues. In their minds, they felt she had overcome disease and dis-ease; she had danced to her own drummer and was moving forward with a dream. They said she rarely complained and had blessed them and many others who called her friend with an unconditional love, enthusiasm, and caring nature. Yet this was a place of grief because one of God's own bright and confident stars had become so down-trodden, so lonesome that she forgot how or chose to no longer trust: *"You are my hiding place; you preserve me from trouble; you surround me with songs of deliverance. I will instruct you and teach you in the way which you should go; I will counsel you with My eye upon you"* (Psalm 32:7–8).

I told them up front, "It's hard to know what to say at a time like this, except there's only one way that this family will get through this trial, will move from this place of deep sorrow to a new place, the next place where the stars will shine again, where forgiveness and hope, peace and familiar reside, and where the sweet and untroubled in life might be restored." I told them that as I prayed for them, it didn't take long for the right words to come, the only ones that would ease their pain and the disbelief. I explained that there are only two words that can do that for anyone, at any time, in any given situation, and those are **Jesus Christ**.

Most importantly and relevant for everyone there that day (and for those reading this today) were Jesus's words from chapter 14 of John, which offer us the ultimate hope for that next place that we all will eventually face: *"Do not let your heart be troubled; believe in God, believe also in Me. In My Father's house are many dwelling places; if it were not so, I would have told you, for I go to prepare a place for you. If I go and prepare a place for you, I will come again and receive you to Myself, that where I am, there you may be also. And you know the way where I am going."*

There isn't much that I know with certainty these days, but I have no doubts that each of us have our times of doubt, are sometimes weak in our humanness, imperfect in the flesh. So was the apostle, Thomas, who doubted and questioned Jesus, *"Lord, we do not know where You are going, how do we know the way?"* (John 14:2). It was Jesus's answer that I wanted everyone in that place to hear that day. I prayed His words would offer them the strength and courage that only Jesus offers; that which I alluded to in the beginning—that *next place* where the stars will shine again, where hope and forgiveness, peaceful and familiar prevail, and where sweet and untroubled might be restored. Jesus's answer for Thomas is the same one that holds true today if we but choose *"The eternal God as our dwelling place."*

"I am the way, and the truth, and the life; no one comes to the Father but through me...Believe Me that I am in the Father and the Father is in Me...Whatever you ask in My name, that will I do, so that the Father may be glorified in the Son. If you ask Me anything in My name, I will do it. If you love Me, you will keep My commandments. I will ask the Father, and He will give you another Helper, that He may be with you forever; that is the Spirit of truth whom the world cannot receive, because it does not see Him or know Him, but you know Him because He abides with you and will be in you. I will not leave you as orphans; I will come to you." (John 14)

It seems that too often these days there are those who are too young to understand, those who are too new to the faith, those too tormented to hear all that the word "death" means or doesn't mean, or those too hardhearted to listen or give Jesus a try. I offered them the one gift, the promise of Jesus Christ, hoping to help them in the awful place they were that they might not fall victim to discouragement or disbelief. It was and remains my prayer that they and others like them from similar experiences might grow in their faith and belief in God so that they have the confidence that He loves them and will be watching over and caring for each of them all the days of their lives if they but call on His Name and then surrender all to Him. It's the only safe place from the torments of hell on earth.

First John 4:8 tells us that God is love and that His love is limitless! If we love those whose lives we touch each day, perhaps they will come to know love and want to pass it on. This [love] is the way God manifests Himself on earth. It's the way I believe that God manifested himself through the community as it gathered together in support of a family during a terrible time and place of overwhelming pain.

Love is the main focus of the only two commandments God sent down with Jesus: *"Love the LORD your God with all your heart, and with all your soul, and with all your mind. This is the great and foremost commandment. The second is like it, 'You shall love your neigh-*

bor as yourself'" (Matt. 22:36–29). It's first God's love that will forever remain a treasure we must hold deeply in our hearts. It's what will sustain us and give us the strength to walk, the courage to keep on keepin' on so that we might overcome life's trials and troubles and hold tight to the promise found in Revelation 2:7: *"To everyone who conquers, I will give permission to eat from the tree of life that is in the paradise of God."*

Until the Cloud Came

He'd been a vigorous, involved man all his life
so the news hit hard when the doctor told him.
Six months wasn't enough time—
he still had plans and pipedreams to pursue,
had a family to love, some fish to catch.
A cloud swept over his soul.

He'd been a man who claimed a blue sky life:
believed in God, felt blessed, knew little strife—
that is until the cloud came.
Grief overshadowed all he trusted before,
so his confidence was left thunderstruck;
he wept like never before.

His doubt and disbelief weren't the darkest—
disrespect for God's mercy and grace
let the thunderstorm plunge in.
His wife perceived his struggles and persevered,
found the courage to persist in God's truth—
saw the darkness dissipate.

She witnessed through his faith under fire,
prayed: with the assurance of the things hoped for,
conviction of things not seen. (Hebrews 11:1)
Prayers were fulfilled when the cloud took him up,
when he yielded his heart up to Jesus,
was received out of her sight. (Acts 1:9)

One Lord, One Faith, One Baptism

*"Peter said to them, 'Repent, and each of you be baptized
in the name of Jesus Christ for the forgiveness of your sins;
and you will receive the gift of the Holy Spirit.'"*

—Acts 2:38

When she first came into our care, she said she'd been raised in a large Catholic family, believed in Jesus Christ, and as the first few days came and went, she demonstrated spiritual comfort and peace. However, as her physical health began to seriously deteriorate, the nurses noted there was something else going on, something that was causing this eighty-nine-year-old woman discomfort. They, of course, tried different medications and doses, different bed positions, back rubs and cool washcloths to her forehead, music therapy, but all to no avail; she became more and more restless, more and more distraught. They called me in.

Their perception was right on because as I sat with her, it didn't take long for her to admit and confess something that had been bothering her for her whole life. She told me she had never been baptized and was worried that meant she was "doomed to hell." She told me her grandparents and parents had moved their family from Austria to America. She said she was the ninth of nine children born to her family and she'd never seen her baptism record, like those all her other siblings had received. She tried to make a joke of it by saying, "I guess with so many kids to worry about they just forgot about baptizing me." However, it obviously was not a joke to her as it was this worry that had remained hidden in her heart, a burden up until this, the end of her life. When I asked why she hadn't gotten baptized as an adult, she simply shrugged and tears rolled down her cheeks— obviously one of those things that got put off. However, in her mind, it was similar to what Jesus experienced, *"I have a baptism to undergo, and how distressed I am until it is accomplished"* (Luke 12:50).

It was through this woman and her desire to be baptized in the name of Jesus Christ that she and I, in separate ways, experienced a mighty work of the Holy Spirit. And it was an astounding experience.

I asked her if she'd like me to call a priest so that she might get this concern of hers corrected. She was familiar enough with Scripture and knew: *"Therefore humble yourselves under the mighty hand of God, that He may exalt you at the proper time, casting all your anxiety on Him, because He cares for you"* (1 Peter 5:6–7). Her response was an immediate and relieved, "Yes!" I called the local parish and learned that the regular priest was on sabbatical but that there was a visiting priest available. He was a kind gentleman, and when I told him the circumstances and asked if there was any way he could help, his answer was also immediate. He came right away.

She asked me to stay with her, so I sat holding her hand while he prepared the elements for Sacrament of the Sick, baptism, and Holy Communion. And then he reached into his bag and pulled out his stole. I noticed it was flowery, embroidered in a beautiful design, unlike anything I'd seen before, and as he began to place it around his shoulders, she spoke to him in a language I didn't recognize. He stopped, looked at her, and responded in a similar dialect. Tears began rolling and she started asking forgiveness through trembling lips.

I sat as observer to one of the most beautiful moments in another human's life as she first repented of her sins, asked forgiveness, and then claimed Jesus Christ as her Savior. The priest and she had spoken to one another in a broken German dialect that he said he remembered from his grandparents, who like hers, had been born in Austria. It was obvious that he was as moved as she was at the circumstances that led him to this woman, on this day, at this time in her life.

Paul teaches in Ephesians 4:4–6, *"There is one body and one Spirit, just as also you were called in one hope of your calling; one Lord, one faith, one baptism, one God and Father of all who is over all and through all and in all." And in 1 Corinthians 12:13, "For by one Spirit we were all baptized into one body, whether Jews or Greeks, whether slaves or free, and we were all made to drink of one Spirit."*

That day, that situation was and remains a most special and perfect example of the love, forgiveness, grace and mercy that God extends to each and every one, if we but ask. What were the odds that day that the one visiting priest would not only be willing to come at a moment's notice, but that he would also know and understand this woman's tradition? It was truly a gift of the Holy Spirit. She was set free through one Lord, one faith, one baptism and crossed over the next day to her eternal home.

Even in This

Once he learned and remembered who I was, and whenever or wherever he saw me, he would raise his right hand and say in a not so quiet voice, "Praise the Lord, Echo, praise the Lord!" And I would repeat back, "Yes, praise the Lord! Always and in everything."

Sometime along the way, we had a serious talk about that *everything* part; as I remember the conversation, he was curious and intent, so we talked about what it meant exactly to praise the Lord in *everything*. Big brown doe eyes quickly turned into a deer in headlights look when he asked, "Even in this (meaning his cancer)?" and I replied, "Yes, even in this."

When he (and most of us are the same), when he didn't understand or didn't want to think about something any longer, he would simply change the subject, as he did that day. But he never forgot what I said, and I was reminded of that when we'd pray together; even and on the evening before he died, when at one point he whispered, "Even in this, Echo?"

"Yes, even in this."

And even on the days when he'd ask a million questions, was bored and just needed someone to sit and talk to him for hours on end, we were all grateful for our time with him. During that period, I was given a beautiful truth by Tia Collins who wrote: *When a special person leaves, one starts to put a heart into words...* and there were and are many words that described not just any ole heart, but the very special heart that was, is, and always will be his.

As I prayed and prepared for his funeral, I came across a writing by Kent Nerburn: "The Sunlight of God." Nerburn wrote: *"When we try to understand God, we are like children trying to hold sunlight in our hands. We recognize the presence of something ineffable and mysterious, but always it eludes our grasp. We know that, at heart, all great spiritual truths contain an utter simplicity, a shimmering depth of meaning that eludes definition and gives life a unity that no amount of analysis or knowledge can ever attain."*[8]

It was not my intention then nor is it with this writing to make him or any human being out to be a saint or even more than he was. But because of how he chose to live, deal with, and accept his lot in life, I, and I believe many others as well, were drawn to him because he not only radiated "sunlight" (with a "u"), but most especially radiated "Sonlight" (this time spelled with a capital "S" and an "o"). In his case, there wasn't any struggle trying to put this man's heart into words. Members of his family, co-workers and friends from his work place, staff and friends from Help for Health Hospice, and the Bible contributed words.

Plus God gave me a tool titled "The Peace Prayer of St. Francis of Assisi."[9] It became the outline, broken down, a way for tying a few simple words from that profound intention with a life and acts completed by one ordinary and unpretentious man's walk. My prayer was and is that together we might all come closer to understanding: the Father who created us and His intention for us, and how He uses each and every one of us for His good purpose; the reason He sent His Son to save us, and how a relationship with Jesus can make all the difference in our lives; as well as the work of the Holy Spirit who guides us as He would have us go if we listen.

Lord, make me an instrument of your peace. Most of us do not live special lives. We seldom get called to make great announcements or perform heroic deeds. In fact, too often we probably go to bed at night wondering whether our actions had any effect or if we're worth anything to anyone. This man, on the other hand, humbly accepted his part and gift and played it out well, doing his part to be an instrument of God's peace. His brothers talked about how shy and withdrawn he was as a child; that is until he went to a

---

[8]. Excerpted from Calm Surrender by Kent Nerburn.
[9]. "The Peace Prayer of St. Francis of Assisi."

children's center for special schooling from where he came home a different person. They said that through the encouragement of others, he became totally confident and fiercely independent, became Mr. Personality. We saw that at the hospice home; he didn't know a stranger and became the unofficial greeter. He would meet and greet patients, their families, and visitors. He would win over even the most resistant who at first weren't sure about this boisterous, come right into your room, individual.

Where there is hatred let me sow love. A plaque of 1 Corinthians 13:4–8 sat on the bookcase in his family home amid a cluster of pictures; reminders of what's most important in this world. It reads: *"Love is patient, love is kind. It does not envy, it does not boast, it is not proud. It is not rude, it is not self-seeking, it is not easily angered, it keeps no record of wrongs. Love does not delight in evil but rejoices with the truth. It always protects, always trusts, always hopes, always perseveres. Love never fails… And now these three remain, faith, hope, and love. But the greatest of these is love."* He came from a family of faith, hope, and love, and he became a sower of faith, hope, and love. When I asked if he was ever sullen or got angry, his mother said, "Not so much." Again, at the hospice home we watched him work—he had the rare ability of getting what he wanted; even if he had to call ten people before he'd find someone to say yes. And he was always grateful for any favor or kindness shown; he enjoyed simple things; took great pleasure in them in fact. His exuberance and love for life was contagious.

Where there is injury let me sow pardon. When we are told to sow pardon, "forgive us our trespasses as we forgive those who trespass against us," God is telling us to seek healing and reconciliation, not approval or even acceptance. That's easier for some than others. He was aware of injury because of the teasing he'd suffered through his life because of his "being different"; he wanted everyone to know peace. I remember an incident where I overheard another male patient get impatient and swear at him one day. I immediately went to him and asked if he was okay. He knew exactly what I was talking about and said, "Yeah, I'm fine. He's just not feeling good today, and it's okay." I don't ever remember hearing an unkind word out of his mouth.

Where there is doubt, faith. Spiritual formation, not spiritual conversion, is the gradual opening of the heart to an awareness of a deeper spiritual truth. Romans 10:17 tells us, *"So faith comes from hearing, and hearing by the word of Christ."* We each are given a sense of God and seeds to sow; they are our gifts of insight, our direction and purpose. This young man's presence, more than his words, challenged me. He was raised up in a home of faith; his feet were set upon the path, and from there he chose to turn his heart toward the light of God and trust in the journey. It is in the living of life with its uncertainties and struggles that we are strengthened in our courage. We then witness or not, and his was a witness of faith and hope in a God he could neither see nor touch. We know it best as *"If you have faith the size of a mustard seed...nothing is impossible to you"* (Matthew 17:20).

Where there is despair, hope. In the last few hours of his life, he was able to and chose to turn from a fear of the unknown to a trust that Jesus was coming to get him. He told me, "I'm ready; I'm not scared anymore; I'm just tired." I shared this to encourage his family then, but indeed all of us as the family of Christ today; the gift of our presence is exactly what a despairing soul needs—no more, no less. His family gathered around him in a faithful and loving vigil; they bore witness to the love they held for this man. He felt that love, opened his eyes and looked in wonder on all of them. And he was no longer afraid. We reassured him that he was a child of God and that he mattered. And he believed.

Where there is darkness, light. *"Our lives are lived in the quiet corner of the ordinary"* (Nerburn). It was most apparent that he was an instrument of God's peace through the wonderful light that many of us were hard-pressed to explain but always felt in his presence. If you hadn't been to the hospice home for a while, he'd call you over for a hug; if he recognized you as you drove by, he'd wave. If he saw you across the store, he'd holler. His was a bright light of friendly.

Where there is sadness, joy. A brother described him as loud, boisterous, funny, and easy to like. Yet, there were those times of sadness, those times when he'd cry and feel overwhelmed with fear. But he never stayed down long. His beautiful nature wouldn't let him. He loved parties, from birthdays to Christmas. He had a favorite place to eat out, no matter the occasion. He had some favorite, famous/perhaps more infamous sayings that made us all laugh. A watch awarded for twenty years of service gave him great joy.

And he loved to be needed and doing. It gave him joy. One of his "chores" at the hospice home was to care for the bird feeders. Staff helped him with the birdseed. One of our favorite stories about him was one day when he was watching the birds and talking about how much they ate, he said, "They are pigs; they're just flying pigs." And then he laughed his great laugh. He was blessed in that life brought him joy! Being the center of attention brought him joy; watching the Broncos play brought him joy; going to spend time with his family brought him joy; somebody bringing him a malt or a huge Mountain Dew full of ice brought him joy; a shoebox full of Special Olympic medals brought him joy; and music brought him joy.

Oh, Divine Master, "The shape of the spiritual vessel we create to receive God will determine the shape of the God we experience" (Nerburn). His faith in Jesus, while childlike in many ways, was a faith immeasurable, constant, and precious. Oh, Divine Master, to have the faith of a child: *"As for you, let that abide in you which you heard from the beginning. If what you heard from the beginning abides in you, you also will abide in the Son and in the Father"* (1 John 2:24).

Grant that I may not seek so much to be consoled as to console. To be understood as to understand. Have you ever worn the pair of shoes known as "Nobody understands?" The feeling of not being understood can become a part of a person's life in a significant way. Over his lifetime, this man struggled with not being understood, and it was significant for him. His family worked to protect him; his friends tried to protect him. Ultimately though, we learned his knowledge and awareness of his situation were more obvious than any of us realized, until the day before he died.

He knew that his condition had changed dramatically, and so he surrounded himself with his family. He asked for the Chaplain to come; I anointed and prayed with him. Native friends came to pray and performed a cedaring ceremony. We all came to understand most clearly that night that he was very aware of and was facing the

Great Unknown with a courage and an inner strength that could only come from the Holy Spirit. He understood it was his time and he whispered to me that he was ready for Jesus "to take me home." He whispered it because he didn't want his family to worry or be sad. "Tell them I'm going to be with Jesus."

To be loved as to love. It is only through love that we feel connected to anything; it is the closest many of us will ever come to feeling holy. He embraced love, shined love, and gave it away freely and without expectation. Oh, how he flourished under its sweet light. Oh, how he shared that sweet light. Whenever I saw him at the home, he would ask if we could pray. He would wait patiently until I finished whatever I was doing. Never once did he ask for prayers for himself; always, always he wanted to pray for someone else, usually someone in the home or someone in his family. He was very aware of what was happening up and down the hall, and so when I'd ask, "Who should we pray for today?" he had a name and a reason.

For it is in giving that we receive. When we give, we are opening the doors and allowing the light of love to shine through. His family, co-workers, and caregivers all made note of the fact that he was aware of those around him. From childhood up, he was aware of needs, maybe from an overheard conversation, and rather than shrug it off or simply ignore it, he chose to do what he could for others. A friend told about a time when she was struggling financially as a single mother and winter was coming; a couple days later, here came this man with a new Broncos winter coat for her youngest son. He loved to give gifts. His brothers said that when he got something in mind to do for someone else, he was relentless, calling everyone he knew who might help him do what needed done.

It is in forgiving that we are forgiven. Think of the miracle of being forgiven. What a gift, and hopefully a sweet reminder that will help each of us from here on out touch the world with a gentler hand. God's forgiveness is something freely granted, neither earned nor deserved; something lovingly offered without thought of acknowledgment or return. It's called grace.

This man was full of grace; gave forgiveness often and seemingly easily.

And it is in dying that we are born to eternal life. There are many ways to die. We can face it with fear and trepidation, or we can face it with hope and trust. What I do know for sure, whatever the case, those left living are changed forever in a most positive way when someone rises above their fear and trepidation. This man knew the way, believed he belonged to the church of God, and easily forgave and as a result was forgiven. Nerburn says, "Our lives are our witness, and our witness is our legacy." This story is that of one simple man who made his choice and as a result, left an amazing legacy of witness to the sunlight and Sonlight of God.

What Was It about Him?

"If you faint in the day of adversity, your strength is small."

—Proverbs 24:10

What was it? What was it about him, one ordinary man who drew us in and kept us coming back for more? More laughs, more jokes, more coffee, cocoa, cookies, and pie, as well as more negativity, more cusswords, more verbal abuse?

He was a curmudgeon—at his quirky best, right out of central casting as the grumpy, bad-tempered, difficult, cantankerous old man. He was also a hardworking, self-described farmer, plain and simple, but all who knew him recognized that he was anything but plain or simple. He had been blessed with a healthy body, a faithful family, and a chosen career as a farmer in a close-knit rural community in which he loved, lived, and thrived. He was enjoying life as a take-charge, very much in control man who had not given much thought to his mortality; that's despite the fact that he worked alongside Mother Nature all his life, saw life and death all around him on a seasonal and consistent basis. The truth is, he was human with all the imperfections that word entails and honestly told me he thought to live "forever, I guess." He was definitely a man who lived life with a gusto second to none.

God had other plans for this partly cantankerous and partly endearing man, and it was only after he was gone and through weeks of thought that we were finally able to come up with our answer to "What was it about him?" The answer had more to do with our growth as caregivers, because he challenged us at every level, than his acceptance of the fact that he was dying.

It was due to a sense of accomplishment and the feeling of approval. If we got him to laugh, say thank you, or were given a nickname, it gave us a sense of accomplishment. These things made us feel like we were doing our job and were good at it. These things made all the hard times with him bearable. We had a hundred opportunities to get his approval throughout the day because he rang his call bell often—sometimes every five minutes even though his daughter just left the room to get him something else from the kitchen. He said once that he wanted to make *sure the girls had enough to do*. Every CNA, staff member, and nurse learned how to make his special cocoa. If we didn't make it right we heard about it. So we did our best to always do it right.

His family was dedicated to him, which in itself was nothing like the staff had seen before. Members of the family would come every morning and night; others would sit all day. They had the same challenges as the staff though, and the emotional abuse was worse for them. Even so, they were present every day.

Once he finally accepted that he was dying, which came after a lot of additional time and work with the counselor and chaplain, he was able to express himself without the anger and negativity. He got to a place of being able to say the words "I love you" to those desperately seeking it. He was able to play games and share stories, all the while drawing all of us further into that mystery of the attraction toward him.

In the end, it came down to the truth that we all felt privileged to be part of his journey. He wrestled long and hard. He became and was most importantly a person we will never forget because his was a successful transition from scared to death of death to acceptance and giving in to what God had in store for him all along. We felt accomplishment when he died peacefully surrounded by his family.

We've decided that God's plans included some teaching that each of us needed to learn that we might grow in our faith, compassion, patience, hope, forgiveness, and acceptance. All we know for sure is that this "toughest SOB I've ever met" was a stubborn, determined, loving, protective, hardworking provider, active member of his community and steward of the land and remained so from his youth until the last days of his life.

He among the many others we've worked with over the years challenged and as a result helped us to become better human beings and caregivers. He didn't faint in his day of adversity and his strength was anything but small. He taught us, *"Let brotherly love continue... remember them that are in bondage...and them that suffer adversity..."* (Hebrews 13:1–3)

Serving a Bigger Picture

"For the word of God is living and active and sharper than
any two-edged sword, and piercing as far as the division
of soul and spirit, of both joints and marrow, and able
to judge the thoughts and intentions of the heart."

—Hebrews 4:12

He'd been raised in an orthodox, traditional church that taught one must work, earn his way to righteousness. As a typical young man he began making choices, had questions, and broke away from that church. In addition, there was one scripture—Hebrews 4:12—that he had painfully taken to heart with a negative implication, one that had never allowed him to forgive himself for certain thoughts, intentions, and choices he'd held or made over the years. In his case, a religious conviction ended up being a barrier to peace and comfort during much of his life but especially so during his first weeks in hospice care.

It seemed he had always been a very sensitive man who was looking for acceptance, love, and approval. He assumed guilt regarding every wrong decision and bad choice he'd made. It was only through the dying process that he was able to openly and honestly admit and talk about this issue and how it had affected his entire life—his personal well-being, his family life, his careers, and indeed, carried over to all aspects.

He began to equate it all to living and dying in Christ after we read 2 Corinthians 13 together one day. By any interpretation, this chapter is a warning, is Paul's final advice that we must examine ourselves—our hearts and intentions. Verse 5 says, *"Test yourselves to see if you are in the faith; examine yourselves! Or do you not recognize this about yourselves, that Jesus Christ is in you—unless indeed you fail the test?"* Verse 6 adds, *"And I trust you will discover that we have not failed the test, except you be reprobates; but I hope you recognize that we have passed the test and are approved by God."*

He began to seriously examine his life through the three different careers he'd held. As a welder, he said he spent much of his time looking down on his work, but added that a skilled welder can do his job upside down or sideways. He never felt skilled, so he only looked "down" on his work. As for his years working for the railroad, he made the comparison between jumping on a train versus the way to properly get on a train, as well as the opposite end of the spectrum which involved getting stuck on a train versus finding a proper way to get off the train. He admitted that depending on the situation, he oftentimes chose to jump on or off rather than properly begin or end something.

He credited that it wasn't until he became a nurse that he finally came to know purpose and was able to take pride in his work and himself. While some of the old heart and intentions interfered from time to time, nursing is when and how he learned he could serve a bigger picture through faith in Christ: *"For by grace you have been saved through faith; and that not of yourselves, it is the gift of God; not as a result of works, so that no one may boast. For we are His workmanship, created in Christ Jesus for good works, which God prepared beforehand so that we would walk in them"* (Ephesians 2:8–10).

Once he began to realize he had been saved through faith, he was able to get better control over his emotions and to recognize, "God gave us emotions for a reason. They are like a song that brings back times. I have control, shed tears or not, allow them to take me back or push them away and do other things." He said, "Emotions help you put everything in place—serve as a photo album of pictures which you can look at one at a time, remember, and then put them back on the shelf."

For him, nursing "WOWED me all the time. Those who were their own person would tell you like it is, like it or not. They were honest. Through patient care you learn to develop rapport and trust." He cherished, "Nursing means touching, in more than one way: skin to skin, heart to heart, and through turning sadness to humor." He said he loved making patients laugh; it was through joking and teasing that he helped people celebrate life and being alive. He told a story about hiding under a patient's bed one night and scaring the nurse who was just coming on duty. She was a stern nurse and the patient was having a hard time with her. His stunt got them both laughing and opened a door for better communication between a nurse and her patient. He said, "Part of being alive is to be teased, to have fun." He added that dealing with people who face disease and dis-ease, who are struggling in their life, was a special challenge for him. He had no qualms holding hands or shedding tears with people. It opened doors to healing on both sides.

The end results of this man's life review of both the bad and the good proved to be restorative. As he came to finally and truly understand that he was accepted, approved, and loved by Christ, he reached a place of peace. At the heart and intentions of this good nurse was a person who honestly set out to make a difference in other people's lives; his was an amazing offering and gift. Once he'd figured out who he was in Christ, he couldn't separate himself from his purpose as a nurse; in his last weeks, he got in the habit of making the rounds with his walker up and down the halls in the hospice home; he would encourage the staff, visit with different patients and/or their family members; he went into one gentleman's room and told him good night every night. At the memorial service we held after his death, that same gentleman spoke of how that one intention made him feel accepted, loved, and approved through his dying process.

All the elements and different experiences of this man's story proved to be such a great metaphor for not only his life, but indeed, for all our lives—how we tend to look "down" on ourselves and our work or life choices; choose to work upside down or sideways; jump onto versus choosing to get on properly so that we, too, might come to the realization that we all serve a bigger picture if we but only take time to examine God's Word. And that's how he chose to finish his life; we spent hours together talking about, praying over and studying Scripture on the subject of living and dying in Christ. In the end, this man's purpose for telling his story was to "serve a bigger picture," and by sharing his heart, he hoped and prayed it might serve someone else and save them some of the grief he'd experienced throughout his lifetime by accepting guilt over God's grace. Together we prayed it would help others hear and remember, *"Jesus said, 'I am the resurrection and the life; he who believes in Me will live even if he dies, and everyone who lives and believes in Me will never die. Do you believe this?'"* (John 11:25–26).

The Assurance of Life

"Faith is the assurance of things hoped for,
the conviction of things not seen."

—Hebrews 11:1

I met him the first time when his wife came into our hospice care. His grief was real and he didn't try to hide it. His heart was breaking but he said he was placing his trust in Christ. I liked his confidence in regard to the assurance of life everlasting. I didn't see or hear from him again for a couple of years, but then he called and asked if I'd officiate a wedding—his wedding. He said he had met someone—an angel—who was widowed also and together they had found a new hope, new comfort, new life. *"For just as the sufferings of Christ are ours in abundance, so also our comfort is abundant through Christ"* (2 Corinthians 1:5). It was a blessing to share in the abundance of love and joy between him and his new and extended family.

The next phone call came a few months later—he was now dealing with his own cancer and his new bride asked if I'd come visit him. A few weeks later I officiated at his funeral. Because this man held onto his faith with such extraordinary confidence, strength, and courage, I was able to say it had been a blessing to know him and shared the following thoughts:

It is my intention that as we work our way through this service today, you'll understand why I use the word blessed in regard to the intimidation, unfairness, uncertainty, and sorrow that comes with the "C" word, and it's all because of the faith, strength, and courage that this man and his family demonstrated. Part of the story was, this man had spent forty years in a wheelchair, paralyzed from the waist down after an accident. For him the simple task of getting up, getting ready, and going to work wasn't so simple. There were a lot of things that he had to do just to get up, let alone get ready for and go through the days, but you never knew it with how he presented himself—always with a presence of strength and determination. All he said was, "Life's not as easy when you can't use your legs."

Despite that, this man didn't let paralysis stop him; his family said he could do anything and build anything. From being a manager of a business, to writing books, hunting, fishing, carving antlers, taxidermy, carpentry, metal fabricating, forging; from A to Z, he could do it. He never let anything hold him back or stop him from doing something. His mantra was, if I can't do something the way I used to, then I simply need to find a new way to get it done. His bride said he lived out an attitude of gratitude: *"This is the day which the LORD has made; let us rejoice and be glad in it"* (Psalm 118:24). Family and friends also used the words fair and integrity when describing him; friends and co-workers alike said he was the type of person whose handshake meant something—his integrity was something you could trust through his handshake.

We heard from him through his own poetry, and about how this not perfect in any way but simple ordinary man chose to live out the time and life he had been given in an extraordinary way, demonstrating an extraordinary strength. I shared a quote that I felt summarized his situation: *"Faith is seeing light with your heart when all your eyes see is darkness."*

He lived under what the rest of us consider tough circumstances: in a wheelchair for 40 years of his life, losing his first wife to cancer, and then his own battle with the disease. Through it all, he refused the word handicapped—refused to get a handicap sticker—and refused the word cancer. He truly believed: *"The LORD is my strength and song, and He has become my salvation"* (Exodus 15:2), and his belief in eternity never wavered.

At the family's request, I read from Jeremiah 29:11–14, *"For I know the plans that I have for you, declares the LORD, 'plans for welfare and not for calamity, to give you a future and a hope.'"* I explained, "If we read just that one statement and take it out of context, we might question: So did God give this man an accident, the death of his wife, and cancer? Where's the hope and future in that plan? We might begin to see and feel intimidation, unfairness, uncertainty, and sorrow, and decide what's so great about God if his plans include disease, pain, suffering?"

But there's more to the story, and he was not only well aware of it but chose to accept it all, not as something God handed him, but that which simply came as a result of our fallen world. He accepted it all as an opportunity to draw nearer to his Lord and Savior. He had the choice, just as we all do. He believed God's plans for us include our seeking and calling upon Him, searching for and coming to Him with all our hearts so that He, our Lord and Savior, can restore and gather us from this world, this temporary place, and take us back home with Him. That's God's plan for us and He promises: *"I will listen for you. I will bring you back to the place from where you came"* (Jeremiah 29:14).

I asked the audience that day and you reading this story now: Do you see what God meant when He spoke through the prophet, *"I know the plans I have for you?"* The question for the living, those left behind is: how is this truth going to affect your comings and goings and choices in the days ahead? It's my forever prayer that every man, woman, and child will give Jesus a chance. His promise, His assurance is found in John 14:1–6, *"Do not let your hearts be troubled; believe in God; believe also in me. My Father's house has many rooms; if that were not so, would I have told you that I am going there to prepare a place for you? And if I go and prepare a place for you, I will come back and take you to be with me that you also may be where I am. You know the way to the place where I am going."* Thomas said to him, "Lord, we don't know where you are going, so how can we know the way?" Jesus answered, *"I am the way and the truth and the life. No one comes to the Father except through me."*

If it hadn't been for cancer, I might not have ever gotten to observe such an amazing show of strength—physical, emotional, and spiritual. As recorded in Mark 12:30, Jesus commanded, *"And you shall love the LORD your God with all your heart, and with all your soul, and with all your mind, and with all your strength."* This man gave the Lord all of his heart—every ounce of strength, grit, and trust he had. In addition, his wife (who had already buried one husband) likewise never wavered; she gave every ounce of strength, lovingkindness, patience, gentleness, and compassion she had to her husband and his family. She proved to be more than his angel; she proved to be a champion caregiver. Now do you understand why I feel so blessed to have met this family? Now do you understand why this story had to be part of this collection about living out and finishing life?

This couple made their choices, walked them out, and in the process taught family, friends, acquaintances, and most especially me how I, too, might walk out the balance of my days so that: *"Hearts may be encouraged, having been knit together in love and full assurance of understanding resulting in a true knowledge of God's mystery, that is, Jesus Christ Himself, in whom are hidden all the treasures of wisdom and knowledge"* (Colossians 2:2).

The Beauty of It All

"One thing I have asked from the LORD, that I shall seek:
that I may dwell in the house of the LORD all the days of my life,
to behold the beauty of the LORD, and to meditate in His temple."

—Psalm 27:4

At the time, his was the briefest but has ever since remained the most confident, comforting, and compelling statement I've ever received from a patient regarding his response to living and dying. It was my introductory visit with this particular gentleman, and as usual, I briefly introduced myself and explained who I was, asked permission to enter his room, and informed him that I needed to ask a few questions for the spiritual assessment. His gentle blue gaze met mine—clearly cooperative. He was accommodating as we began our conversation and he answered my few queries straightforwardly.

As we talked, he briefly explained his involvement in a faith system, his beliefs as a Christian, and expressed his lack of fear and the reasons he held hope for a future. We talked about my coming around for regular visits, and he was agreeable to that idea and also helped me determine a Plan of Care that would serve him best while receiving hospice services. While not able at the time to define why, I immediately felt comfortable in his presence.

After getting the basics taken care of, I told him I had one more question to ask and it is what I refer to as the "tough question"—specifically, "You've just been given a terminal diagnosis; how are you coping with this?" He turned to look out the window as he considered, but then turned back and obligingly, honestly and humbly said, "Honey, I've always tried to find the beauty in life, no matter the circumstances or situation. I'm not a man to get angry, hold grudges, or harbor regrets; I've always tried to look for the beauty." He turned back to the window in his reflecting before replying, "And I'm trying to honor that by looking for the beauty in this too."

Ecclesiastes 3:11 came alive for me in a whole new way with the realization, *"God has made everything beautiful in its time."* And therein was the answer to why I immediately felt at ease in this man's presence. This was a person who truly had asked the Lord that he might dwell in His house all the days of his life so that he might: *"Build himself up in his most holy faith, and behold the beauty of keeping himself in the love of God, waiting patiently for the mercy of our Lord Jesus Christ to bring him to eternal life"* (Jude 20–21).

Confident, comforting, compelling—I couldn't think of a better story or way to conclude a book about living and finishing life in the eternal hope: *"Surely goodness and lovingkindness will follow me all the days of my life, and I will dwell in the house of the Lord forever"* (Psalm 23:6).

Looking for Golden Threads

A mosaic is a conversation
between what is broken and redesigned
in a pattern through the play of light.
A mosaic is a conversation with time:
a narrative arranged and rearranged
o'er the Old and New Testament eras,
seeking beauty in all things common,
creating lines side by side as in rhyme.

Mosaic is a metaphor for life
when out of randomness comes created order.
And although imperfect, man finds beauty
crafted out of community.
From issues shaping our world today
comes allegory aligning progress—
a kinship between our paved-over souls
and being part of something bigger than us.

And so it was and is in our broken world,
we stand on a descending staircase,
daring to ask, "Can we have a change of heart?"
and, "How do we translate God's amazing Grace?"
We've too long met silences among us
but as we enter into the mosaic of life,
the paradox, if we seek unity in all
we'll find dignity's presence, beauty sublime.

The pattern is the thing, the play of light
if we live our lives looking for golden threads,
perceiving and receiving, We are not alone
but belong to a vibrant web of love.
Finding beauty in a broken world is
the work of daring and inspires action.
It's not knowing how much we are needed
but believing beauty belongs to everyone.

Finishing It Well

"I do not consider my life of any account as dear to myself, so that I may finish my course and the ministry which I received from the Lord Jesus, to testify solemnly of the gospel of the grace of God."

—Acts 20:24

As I have considered the stories that "made it" into this collection, I realize there were more positive and hopeful stories than the other. That has been my experience as a human being and hospice chaplain—there are more positive and hopeful stories in our world than the daily news would have us believe. However, the other side exists. Not everyone dies peacefully, gracefully, or comfortably. Those times are a puzzle and a burden that we in the profession endure; they are the stories that I must accept as: "It was what it was." While both attitudes encompass the whole of life, I've found that "finishing life well" boils down to ***choice***.

In my efforts to serve those in hospice care and do it well, I have made choices. I have made and will continue to make mistakes, experience missteps and misread situations. I have spent time with people who do not get the storybook ending, don't find peace as they finish life. The actuality is, it's their experience, not mine, and I'm reminded often that I am merely a servant, not the Savior. The opposite of this is also true: when everything goes well and the person passes peacefully and comfortably and the family experiences comfort from our care, none of us can take any credit for that either. God's Holy Spirit deserves that glory!

For me, doing it well (hospice care and life for that matter) comes down to an ethical and spiritual framework under which I live, work, and breathe. I choose to hold the belief that to most fully and authentically affirm life we must embrace all of life, which includes dying, death, and grief. I believe that every human being deserves loving care and support as they make the transition from this life to the next and their family members and friends deserve loving care and support in their own and separate grief. For me, the transition is above all about respect for the gift of life and the gift of hope for life eternal because of Jesus Christ, *"Blessed be the God and Father of our Lord Jesus Christ, who according to His great mercy has caused us to be born again to a living hope through the resurrection of Jesus Christ from the dead, to obtain an inheritance which is imperishable and undefiled and will not fade away, reserved in heaven for you..."* (1 Peter 1:3–4) Two very special people helped me most clearly recognize and remember this truth as they picked and then chose how they were going to go about finishing life well. And by that I mean making a choice and then going forward in faith and with confidence of the outcome.

First, she was a person I had known for years and counted as a friend. We were the same age and mid-sixties is considered young by many standards, and while we didn't phone each other or get together for lunches, we had mutual friendships in common and knew just enough about each other to trust and respect one another and forgive and forget. The lines of communication had fallen through the cracks of busy lives and so when I heard she had cancer, I was most sad to learn she was already in hospice care with another hospice agency; however, because she asked for my spiritual support, it was without hesitation that I went to her bedside.

As I sat with her and her family members, I listened to their words, their expressions of grief. Some were accepting of her choice not to have any treatment for her cancer and that she was dying. Some were angry that she "wasn't willing to at least try something to stop it." Most were simply ambivalent: hurting, sad, confused, grieving. All expressions and emotions were valid.

As I sat, listening to the differing aspects of conversations in a house full of heartbroken people, I found myself humbly reflecting on why I believe what I believe, and the word choice. I asked one of her siblings, "Why is she so adamantly opposed to treatment of any kind?" The story was she'd observed and walked alongside a neighbor through her emotional and physical suffering with cancer. The doctors told the neighbor she had three months to live and despite all the treatments they tried, not to mention the subsequent pain, she still died within three months. None of the medical interventions helped, and in fact, in my friend's opinion, had ruined the quality of her neighbor's last weeks of life on earth.

So my friend chose to lean on her faith in God's Word and assurance and walk out her final days as they came to her: *"Therefore, being always of good courage, and knowing that while we are at home in the body, we are absent from the Lord—for we walk by faith, not by sight—we are of good courage, I say, and prefer rather to be absent from the body and to be at home with the Lord"* (2 Corinthians 5:6–8).

A few weeks later, another individual expressed a similar attitude by demonstrating a remarkable "faith under fire" which further made me humbly contemplate why I do what I do, why I believe what I believe. As one symptom after another seemed to be attacking his entire body, he faced a big decision: Do I opt to go work with yet another team of doctors, go for more treatment, or do I stop and allow God's will to be done?

Despite his wife's requests to get another opinion, his children's desires that he "try everything possible," and the well-intentioned questions from friends, he drew from his faith. His response to everyone's fears and worries, "Hey, if the good Lord comes to take me home now, I'm the better off; if he leaves me here for a while longer, I'm good with that, too. Either way I'm going to be fine. It's a win-win situation." End of discussion.

And his was perhaps the most humbling and yet instrumental for my growth as a human and Christian because it challenged me at every level. I, who profess to believe in and trust Jesus Christ as my Savior was forced to sit quietly and once again consider the word choice as this man articulated his.

Today, I recognize that these two people and indeed every person from every story in this book gave me a most precious gift in life. Their faith or lack thereof helped me face mine, look myself square in the eye, study my own heart. The question(s) that arose from all of these experiences with these dear souls taught me so much about the vitality of life. In the end and after much reflection and time in prayer, their stories facilitated my learning to keep my focus, my thinking on an ultimate truth, that we all have been given a choice in life, can choose to not or to walk in the trust of a Savior, *"Father, if You are willing, remove this cup from Me; yet not My will, but Yours be done."* As a daughters and sons of our most High Lord God, they made their choices in life and lived with those choices. I am most grateful that ultimately, most of them chose to finish well—enduring valiantly, confidently, and honestly. Praise the LORD!

About the Author

Echo Klaproth is a fourth generation Wyoming rancher who initially began writing to pay tribute to her family's unique heritage. Her early writing reflects the legacy of: family, life's joys and struggles, gains and growth as a daughter of Christ, as well as the blessings she experiences because she was born and raised in Wyoming among good and honest folks. She has published five collections of a unique genre known as cowboy poetry and prose: *Echoes of Days Gone By*, *Echoes in the Wind*, *Words Turn Silhouette*, a CD recitation titled *A Nameless Grace*, and edited an anthology about the genre, *Scattered Lasting Remnants*.

Echo retired from teaching secondary English in 2009 and was ordained a minister of the gospel of Jesus Christ in 2010. She serves as the women's leader at Cornerstone Community Church and as chaplain with Help for Health, a nonprofit hospice organization in Fremont County, Wyoming. *A Requiem to the Vitality of Life* comes from the years and encounters with people as they have lived out and finished their life experience. This collection of writing prayerfully reflects their response to the love of Christ or not and her commitment to Christ and people, and her joy for life. She and her fisherman husband live on a small farm on Boysen Reservoir near Shoshoni, Wyoming.